MW01169897

Ten Balloons

Principles of Leadership, Life and Love

Michael Nygren

SPECIAL THANKS TO

My wife Sherri for helping me give birth this "third child" of ours. I cherish the memories of living out these concepts together for over four decades.

My children and their spouses, Andrea and Eric, Adam and Nikki, and our three amazing grandchildren, Savannah, Hayden and Tyler, who have influenced my life for the better. They have made me rethink our purpose statements over and over.

The individuals who contributed their personal "Balloon Stories" for this book. I liked my book before, but your stories made me love it.

Mary Mathias Dickerson, Assistant Professor of Art, Lee University, for her art in creating the cover that tells the story without words.

Kate Johnsen for the right challenges at the right time in the creating and editing process.

Ten Balloons: Principles of Leadership, Life and Love © 2014
by Mike Nygren

Scriptures taken from the NIV Version of the Bible

Cover Design by Mary Mathias Dickerson

ISBN-13:9781497507135

Published: Tipp City, Ohio

mike@tenballoons.com / www.tenballoons

Editor's Thoughts

My story starts in my early teens, when I had a young youth director who, in his own faith story says that he wasn't quite sure where he was leading that group, but we sure had a good time! Fast-forward fifteen years and he is leading one of the most innovative student ministry groups in the country, at the church I now attend. I marvel at the confident students and young leaders who came out of that ministry. Fast-forward another twenty years and he finally decides to write *Ten Balloons*, which I believe is his wisdom for generations to come.

I was a little star-struck when he asked me to edit his work. But I put on my professional hat and gave it to him straight. He embraced the challenge. And we began.

Absorbing his philosophy as I've worked with each word has allowed me to deeply internalize the life messages of a man whose ministry and influence I've only admired from the fringe. Mike's lessons, and the stories of those who have embraced his life lessons in their own lives, have changed my views. I'm ready for adventure, seeing my friends and primary relationship differently, considering how my balloons need to shift to make better sense in my life.

How will I make a difference in my children's lives? How can I create a relationship with my future grandchildren so they leave the earth better than they found it?

I promise, *Ten Balloons* will make you think. It will inspire you. It will make you uncomfortable at times. It will change you. But aren't we all ready for a little challenge?

Katy Kyle Johnsen, editor, Tipp City, Ohio

Ten Balloons Chapters

Mike's Purpose Statements

Family   *Live life with no regrets.*

Career   *Never take myself or my career too seriously.*

Mental   *Look backward. Look forward.*

Financial   *Give. Save. Enjoy.*

Hobbies   *Have some.*

Primary Relationship   *Be the best.*

Adventure   *Live life and take others along.*

Education   *Learn whatever I have to learn to do whatever I want to do.*

Friends   *Be one.*

Physical   *Give up some things so I can gain everything.*

Introduction

I was a junior in college when my mother died. I was in my dorm when I got the phone call from my dad. The call was not unexpected—it was just a matter of when the cancer would take its final toll. I grew up in the Catholic Church in Brooklyn, New York. I was an altar boy, attended eight years of Catholic school, and still felt ill prepared to receive the news. I was 500 miles away when she died, making it impossible for me to be there when the doctor told my dad the news, which only heightened the feeling of *"life's not fair"* in my mind.

That evening as I lay in bed, I remember crying while dozing in and out of sleep. Sometime in the night I awoke with a wet pillow. After that day my life and understanding of family would change forever. My mother's death became a bittersweet moment.

Living Life So There Can Be No Regrets

It was not uncommon for me to work through my thoughts by asking myself questions. I engaged in this *"self-talk"* particularly at night, when my thoughts seemed to roam in endless directions. The first question I asked myself was, *"Why are you crying, Mike?"* To this day I realize that question might have been the stupidest thing I have ever said. *"Because my mother just died"* was all I could think of saying back to myself. *"Do you think that is what your mother would want right now?"* and, of course, that question was way too deep for me.

Those questions were stuck in my mind. What would my mother say? I am sure she knew she was dying, and that she would not see me again. Then I really started to dig deeper. Would she be mad because I had not been there for three months? Or would she say, *"You belong in school?"* Would she have wanted me to transfer? Skip a semester? Or simply just do something else so that I would be there for her last days? The answer to those questions all came down to a simple *"No."* She and my dad never went to college, and I was fulfilling a dream not only of hers, but of my first generation, immigrant grandparents as well.

Then I realized what she might say, or maybe what I hoped she might say. I knew I had always been a different kind of son as I was growing up. My parents taught me all about respect; I never had any extreme times of talking back, being disrespectful, or making them embarrassed about me. I could have long conversations with my mom. Those were mostly just about stuff— not earth-shattering stuff, but about day-to-day life. In high school I realized one quality about my dad that did not always make for a happy household. He did not enjoy going out to eat and would always much rather eat at home. Whenever we did eat out, it was a special treat. Then I realized that my mom never really got to go out all that much. She, like he, worked a forty-hour week and always looked forward to the weekend.

I am not sure how it began, but somehow about once a month my mom and I would go out to dinner at the local Asian restaurant. An idea she absolutely adored. I, of course, loved the *"free dinner"* out, but I remember never once seeing another mom and son pairing at one of the tables. Thinking back, I guess I suffered from a bit of peer pressure and was probably hoping no one would ever see me with my mom. We had established a tradition that continued throughout my high school career, for which I am very thankful now.

After thinking about my memories with her, I then said to myself, *"What would you do differently, Mike, if she had lived longer?"* The answer was simple. I would have kept on treating her with the same respect and shown the same love I had while she was alive. And of course, taken her out to dinner more often!

I don't remember crying at the funeral. By then, for me, it was a celebration of her life and the relationship that we had. I wished we had had more time together, as I am sure she did. But one thing I know, our relationship had always been good and could not have been much better, at least from the perspective of a nineteen year old.

As time went on, I made a promise to myself about family. I promised that whoever may die in the future I would be able to say the same things. So with Sherri, the children and the grandchildren I live my life not talking about the things we will someday do, but instead living so I will not have regrets in the future. I have never once thought about changing the vision of my family balloon, *"Live life with no regrets."*

Chapter One   **The Ten Balloons**

One evening an old Cherokee Indian told his grandson about a battle that goes on inside people. He said, *"My son, the battle is between two 'wolves' inside us all. One is Evil. It is anger, envy, jealousy, sorrow, regret, greed, arrogance, self-pity, guilt, resentment, inferiority, lies, false pride, superiority and ego. The other is Good. It is joy, peace, love, hope, serenity, humility, kindness, benevolence, empathy, generosity, truth, compassion and faith."* The grandson thought about it for a minute and then asked his grandfather, *"Which wolf wins?"* The old Cherokee simply replied, *"The one you feed."*

A few summers ago I was excited watching my grandson Hayden as we visited the Museum of the Cherokee in Cherokee, North Carolina. At age ten he was happy to see some of his Grandpa Bowlin's heritage and proud to be part Cherokee. It only seemed fitting to begin this book with an illustration for children to show how we each have a choice of our own destiny by the decisions we make in our thinking. In time those choices will impact the way we live.

Why Now?

The chapters ahead are all about the choices we make each day in living a full life. I never imagined that one day I would find a Scripture that would be the foundation of this book. *"I have been young, but am now old" (Psalm 37:25).* If someone told me years ago that I would love growing old, I would not have understood. I have found, though, that this season of my life gets more amazing and fulfilling each day. When I started writing the book, I wondered, why now? Why would I want to tell these stories now? Does wisdom really come from growing old? Is there really a story that needs to be told? I realized the principles in this book are not accidental, but are the result of people investing in me throughout my life. Each of us encounters people who have made lasting impressions and we become who we are through a series of events. So this is a story of my journey and some of the people along the way who have had an impact on my life.

I decided that if I were writing a book about being a CEO of a Fortune 500 company I would research and find industry leaders to help tell the story for my book. This led me on a quest to find people who have already wrestled with the issues of the Ten Balloons and would be willing to tell stories of their journeys.

The great part about living a life focused on the balloons is it is for everyone. I begin teaching this in schools at the fifth-grade level but realize that within families the principles begin to unfold much sooner. I envision this book:

- As a manual for grandparents to evaluate how they can share their own wisdom with their families,

- As a checklist for parents to determine what they believe and decide if their daily life matches their purpose,

- As a plan book for young people who want to create a life that sets them apart from most of their peers.

Each day we watch as our culture is changing—some for the good and some for the bad. I see things like technology and how great it can be—but I also see that it is not so great—and I can see the toll it can take on family and relationships. The list is endless of *"the way things used to be"* compared to the world that we live in today.

I Believe That We Were Each Created for Greatness

My hope is to challenge the readers and to help them see that life is intended to be great and not just ordinary. Some say we are complex people—I think of us as *"complete."* I would like to take you back to when I was young to begin the story of the *Ten Balloons.*

I entered the teaching and coaching profession four decades ago, with a vision and a passion to invest my life doing what I loved to do. My goal hasn't changed—just the venues and the roles that I've had over the years. The primary motivation for this book is to continue my passion in a new venue and for a new audience. I have been blessed with a life of teaching in the classroom, coaching on the track, speaking to audiences, preaching in the Church, running businesses and creating nonprofits. My purpose has always been to help individuals find ways to *"unlock God-given potential."*

So why stop now? The majority of my teaching and coaching centered on the concept that I call Ten Balloons. In need of a visual illustration for an audience of two hundred high school students, I decided on taking the principles I wanted to teach and writing each one on a balloon. The students I was about to address were leaders within their school and communities. My focal point was easy: what does a good leader look like?

Two Sets of Helium-Filled, Multicolored Balloons

The first set had ten helium-filled balloons of different sizes—the smallest being the size of a tennis ball and the largest the size of a basketball. The second had one balloon as close to *"popping size"* as possible, and two others half that size. The rest were inflated two days before to make sure that they would be withering and close to the floor for my presentation. I placed the balloons on opposite sides of the stage, and my first question to the audience was:

Which One Are You?

A question like this is a great way to get the attention of audiences, for sure. I quickly explained how we have choices in life of whom we follow. I asked whom were they following when it came to the sets of balloons.

So often in training we learn about skills, we learn new techniques as leaders, but we are rarely asked, *"Who are we when no one is looking?"* I explained to the students the idea of the Ten Balloons is about how we dream and how we live out our lives to become all that we can be.

The Ten Balloons is an in-depth look at ourselves and what we believe, and what we want to become. It is an intense study of who we are, and who we are as leaders. Unless you live alone on a remote island there will be many times in life where you are a leader or may be called to be a leader. One of my favorite ways to describe a leader is *"one who has followers."*

If that is true, then what kind of leader—or person—have you chosen to be? The one with one big balloon—or the one who attempts to live a more balanced life and has all of the balloons inflated to some degree?

What Ten Balloons Make For A Balanced Life?

That answer, I believe, is up to each individual. It can be more or less than ten balloons, depending on what values are important to you. I landed on the number *ten* because I believe it meets the needs of most of my audiences.

- Adventure
- Career
- Education
- Family
- Financial
- Friends
- Hobby
- Mental
- Physical
- Primary relationship

I list the Ten Balloons alphabetically as to not influence anyone about which one is the most important. What you will find in reading *Ten Balloons* is that it is your life and your future—and how you *"inflate"* your balloons is your decision.

The number one question is always, *"Are you happy with how your balloons are inflated?"* As you deal with this topic, consider two important goals:

- Do not try to make the Ten Balloons all the same size—some areas of our lives will always have higher priority.

- Work to keep the Ten Balloons off the floor— giving just a little attention to all of our balloons makes us more confident and better able to keep all of our balloons afloat!

Friends Along Our Journey!

As I contemplate the Ten Balloons and all the areas of my life, and how I try and manage my own balloons, I can't help but notice that my Friends Balloon is really inflated. I have been blessed throughout the years with so many great friendships and people, that it has trickled into all the various areas of my life. As I look back at my own experience in high school, being that awkward teen, trying to fit in and find my way into various groups, I see that I learned much about humor, making people laugh and finding ways to connect with others.

I focused so much on friendships in school that it appears I would befriend just about any personality. I would try to focus on something I liked about them to find a way to just relate. I was fortunate to have witnessed what this looked like during my time in a youth group. As I got older I noticed that I continued to do the same thing. Look for ways to connect and encourage others. Those traits really helped me to become a better person, and I feel in my current job have helped me to connect with and lead others.

I am almost 30 years out of high school now. As I have gone through my own journey, I have always been amazed at how many great people I have been surrounded by. I find that many of my relationships have helped shape my children, and definitely have taught me along the way. These friendships have led me into various career opportunities and carried me through some of my own life challenges. I know that it is important to inflate all our balloons, and ensure that we spend a bit of time focusing on each, but I can surely attest that without focusing on this balloon, not sure I would be able to balance all the others so well.

Randy, Logistics manager, Kentucky

Why Is There No Spiritual Balloon?

Having no spiritual balloon is a very conscious decision on my part. Although I have lived (and worked) nearly my entire life in the Church, I have seen great harm from having a separate spiritual balloon. If you consider yourself a *"person of faith,"* then I believe it is important to base your purpose statement for each of your balloons on your faith. Just as each of us chooses which are the most important areas of our lives, I believe that how we live out our lives can be a barometer of our faith.

I have seen the failure of the spiritual balloon when people base their success of it: on how often they pray, go to church, tithe, or how involved they are in the church ministries. Although those might all be essential to one's faith, it is possible to neglect our primary relationship, our family or any other of the balloons while serving at church. The importance of faith in your life will influence how you create the vision for your balloon. A simple illustration is your financial balloon. What would God desire you to do with your money? Is it just tithing to the church? What about saving? What about the percentage not saved or given away—what stewardship would be required? If I am a parent—what am I teaching and modeling to my children about money?

I have watched with tragic results where there was a Faith Balloon. Teens often do not have their own faith, but instead live on the expectations of their parents and faith community. Unfortunately when they leave home or the church of their formative years they sometimes give up that balloon — but in reality they still are making life decisions based on their faith without realizing it. Often students go off to college or the military and *"cannot find a place to worship."* They believe that their spiritual balloon has been deflated, and yet that is often not the case, as they have been living faith through all areas of their lives.

Balloons Pop!

I chose the idea of Ten Balloons for a reason. Balloons pop. Some are popped intentionally, and some are popped by accident. Some pop because they get too much air (attention), and some fall to the floor because of a lack of air (attention). It is always fun to pop one of the balloons in the middle of the presentation to emphasize the *"shock"* of what can happen as the air is quickly let out of a balloon in our lives.

For a moment let's think ahead to the career balloon. Imagine for a moment that you lose your job today. Imagine that you had the three inflated balloons and the other seven were in some need of attention. The one that popped today was your career.

For most people in the workforce the loss would seem devastating. How will I pay the bills? What will I do now? What will people say? After the initial shock what is next? How long can I be without a job? What if I need to go to school again? Will we lose our home?

When a balloon pops, there are usually no easy solutions but there are some possibilities. What if the other nine balloons are where you needed them to be? You may have money in the bank to sustain you despite the loss. Your family could provide emotional, and possibly financial help. You may have a network of friends who might have connections to new opportunities. You might have a hobby that you had wanted to someday turn into a business. You might be relieved you lost the job because it was no good for your health. You might have needed a switch but were scared to quit. It might have been time to take that needed adventure. I don't want to make it sound like it is not a big deal to lose a job—but it is a matter of putting your life in perspective. We all know of people who have changed careers only to explain, *"I should have done it sooner."*

What If A Balloon Pops?

What if your primary relationship balloon is about your spouse? What if it popped? The reality is that in our culture today it is predicted that half of all marriages will end in divorce. The initial response to divorce is often traumatic, and the questions about how we will go on are endless. What about the children? What about money? What about the future?

At some point we are hopefully able to put things into perspective. The first question should always be, how are the other nine balloons? How are my relationships? How are my finances? What are my career options? How will the children cope?

And so it goes with the balloons. We never want to predict that disaster or hard times will come our way—but for most, life will deal us some popped balloons. Although we can never really be fully prepared for that event, we can at least understand the need to invest in more than just two or three or four balloons.

Chapter Two The Logic Of The Balloons

Living a life based on the Ten Balloons is founded on the idea that we are created to be multifaceted individuals. We each have the potential—and the choice—of living a healthy, happy, balanced and passionate life. The Ten Balloons:

- Are never to be confused with personal goal-setting
- Require that you take time for reflection, conversation and prayer to define your purpose statement for each balloon
- Are designed as a tool to help set annual and seasonal goals once your purpose statement is created
- Will evolve and morph in the different seasons of life
- Should be short statements that define you as a total person
- Should never be adopted from other peoples' purpose statements

The Difference Between Goal-Setting And Purpose Statements

A simple illustration to explain the difference between goal-setting and purpose statements can be seen in the evolution of my own life balloons.

My 2014 Adventure Balloon Purpose Statement

To continue to live a life based on adventure, and bring as many people along as possible

Having a firm grasp on this as my purpose statement, I evaluate the goals that I want to set in the upcoming year. It is important to consider the merging of people and ideas from my other nine balloons. My 2014 goals then evolved through asking myself a series of questions:

- Where will Sherri and I travel?
- What new adventures will we attempt?
- Where we will travel with the entire family?
- What adventure traditions will we renew?
- Who can I reconnect with from my past through adventure?
- Where will our three weeks of adventure with the grandchildren be?
- What age-appropriate dreams must we include for the grandchildren?
- What new photo adventure books will I create?
- With World Changers, what opportunities will we create?
- How many new people can we involve through World Changers in travel and adventure?
- How can I add adventure with the staff at showpig.com?
- How can I help coach people with their adventure balloon?

Looking at my list of questions and topics for just one of the balloons helps to explain why it requires time, reflection, conversation and prayer to define your purpose statement in each area. I usually spend the month of December reflecting about what happened during the year and then begin the process of dreaming and thinking ahead for the upcoming years.

I would like to take you back about thirty years to my adventure balloon as our children were growing up, and let you see how purpose statements must be rethought each year.

My 1970s Adventure Balloon Purpose Statement

Travel with our children as much as possible on a teacher's salary

I hope you can see what I mean by the morphing of purpose statements when you compare my two. Did we have fun in the '70s, even with such a limited vision? Enough that I could write another book about the many opportunities we had with a *"Backdoor Travel"* mindset.

- We never let the fact that we were often living paycheck to paycheck limit our vision on adventure.
- We made the decision to keep adventure as part of our family expenses, just as we would our food bill and our house payment.
- We knew that postponing travel until we could afford it meant it would never happen.
- We knew that our kids would only be young once, and therefore we wanted to let them see and experience as much of the world as we could afford.

How Does Creating Your Ten Balloons Work With A Spouse?

Just as there are no right and wrong answers about which balloon should be the largest or the smallest, there are also no rules of how you incorporate the Ten Balloons into marriages. For Sherri and me it has become more of a tradition that Sherri asks, *"Well, what are we doing this upcoming year?"* It is not that she does not care; it is that for forty-four years I have taken the lead in this area and it has worked. Part of Sherri's DNA would not be to write out her statements, but instead let them evolve as needed through the seasons of her life.

Years ago, I introduced a fellow youth worker to the Ten Balloons. Greg was already a serious goal-setter and very successful in life, he embraced the idea of taking the time to wrestle with finding his purpose statements. Years later, when I met up with Greg, he explained with great joy and confidence how he and Cara still built their lives around the balloons. He explained how they travel to New York City all alone each winter, to continue to refine their purpose statements and goals. They use the time away to focus on what they want to accomplish in the future for themselves and their children.

In the mid-'70s, when I became serious about this process of writing out mission statements and goals, I studied what Zig Ziglar had to say about the topic. The first time I heard him speak, he explained how he knew from past experiences that only three percent of the audience would take him up on the challenge of writing out goals in many areas of life and then working toward achieving them. I was taken aback by his numbers, and, given the opportunity, might have disagreed with him on that. As time went on, that number was imbedded in my thinking, and for each audience I try to imagine who may be in the three percent. Over time I have found his three percent prediction to unfortunately be very accurate.

Creating mission statements is hard work. I wish I could say it is easy, but it is not. What I realize, though, is the consequence is great for not taking the time to do this hard work. When people are honest about their lives, they will usually tell you about the balloons they have that they wish had either more or less air in them. Yet knowing that, most people are content in the routines they have established and can justify away any of the hopes and dreams that they wish they could accomplish.

A great starting point for most people is to find someone who would also like to establish the Ten Balloons as a lifestyle and begin a conversation. Some people will tell you that you must have an accountability partner to make this happen, and for some that might be true. I think the greatest thing might be to find someone who will encourage you, listen to some of your ideas, but most of all, that they will realize that you are in that very small percentage and just need some encouragement from someone who believes that you can succeed.

Chapter Three   The Family Balloon

The concept of family today is drastically different from how it looked when I was growing up. The four of us ate dinner together every night. My grandparents lived down the street. Not one of my friends in junior high or high school came from a divorced home. Our collective lives were not crazy busy.

The starting point for anyone in thinking about a balanced family life is what I call thinking *"both ways."* I explain to students that they need to be as concerned with their younger brothers' and sisters' as they are with their own future. I also tell of the need for them to make good choices. I tell them my mother's story, and I know for many it has had a lasting impact.

Parents need no reminder to invest in their children, and probably not even a reminder that their parents are getting older and have a new set of needs. For grandparents I ask one of the hardest questions imaginable, *"Do you really need to move away from your children and grandchildren and start a new life with new friends somewhere else?"* It is not a fun question, but a question that probably should be asked more often. That cultural concept is a part of the *"me generation,"* and the cost is high with a divorce rate approaching fifty percent. Grandparents sometimes forget that they have an opportunity to offer stability and wisdom in this time of transition for all. Although it might be good to live in a warmer climate, eat dinner at 4:00 p.m., invest heavily in the medical community, and Skype with the family, I believe that God might have intended a greater role of influence for those in their retirement years.

Beginning to create a purpose statement with family can be hard. As children and grandchildren grow through different seasons, it becomes easy to just play a reactive part in their lives. When you take time to consider all the balloons, you see how family can truly be woven into all areas of life, and then the priority of family *"looking both ways"* becomes much clearer.

The Dynamics Of Divorce

How do you explain to your children that you are getting a divorce? Since there isn't an instruction book that came with the wedding vows, each family responds in its own way. I could write another book about sitting across the table from a teenager who is working through their parents' divorce. The teens' perception of the impact is usually on hundred and eighty degrees away from their parents'. Most commonly, parents tell me how *"It is all working out and the children are adjusting to the situation."*

I am sure that is true for some, but I have met with many young people when their worlds have just been turned upside down. From their perspective no one else really cares about them, but instead about each of the parents' agendas. I have worked with some of the best students ever, and many are thriving within a divorced framework. I believe that the difference is in the parents being honest.

"My Dad's Work Balloon Is Gigantic!"

At the heart of this book, and why I began teaching this in a fairly aggressive way, is a response to what I heard from students as they explained their perception of their parents. For so many the teens viewed their fathers as having an extremely large career balloon, and most of the time ignoring or denying the change needed in the other areas of their lives.

Interestingly enough, both the guys and girls would overwhelmingly explain that Mom, including moms working outside the home, had balloons that looked nothing like Dad's. The perception was that even though Mom worked a full-time job, she was still responsible for keeping all the balloons inflated in her own life as well as the balloons of the rest of the family. They explained Dad more with the idea that because his focus was on career — he was interested in the financial balloon, which, in turn, meant he provided for the family. Most did not buy into Dad's justification.

Talking with students honestly about how they view each parent was something they welcomed doing. It was not so much that they wanted to complain—maybe it was to understand—but most importantly to grasp the unique influence each parent had on them. Through teaching the balloons, I always found students being extremely confident in their own future based on coming away with the strengths of their parents instead of focusing on the things that were not happening.

I believe working through the Ten Balloons is one of the greatest premarital strategies in the world. When working with couples, I first give them a quick overview of the concept and a little about what each balloon might include. I then challenge them to independently write out a vision statement for each balloon without showing it to one another or talking about it. When we meet again, I serve as the moderator as they unpack some of what they are thinking in each area.

There are always some moments of tension during our time together—but the foundation for the family balloon is built around what we believe about the other balloons and blending them with our spouses. Looking back on our marriage, I don't have a clue what our marriage counseling was about. I continue to be passionate about the balloons, wishing someone would have asked us questions about real life, real dreams, and what we believed the future could be together.

Our Marriage Comes Before Our Kids

I met my husband at Taco Bell when I was 18. My friend Carey and I were walking in, and he was going through the drive-thru. Isn't that where all people meet their spouse? I had big plans, leave for college, change the world through an afterschool reading program, live in New York City and get married at 30.

While in high school I was challenged to make a list of what my perfect husband would look like, and I was pretty good at sticking to the list. Steve kept coming around, and we had so much fun together. He supported me and encouraged me in every endeavor. He met every requirement on my list—except one. I was fearful of marrying someone from a broken home. I was blessed with an amazing family heritage that encompassed the meaning of family and marriage. I learned about lifelong commitment by watching my parents, grandparents, and great-grandparents. I just loved my life and couldn't imagine anything different for my future children.

Fast forward.

That summer I was working in the inner city of Cincinnati. Unlike most 19-year-old guys Steve showed up all the time to play with those kids, and I saw he really loved them. I can remember it like it was yesterday. I looked back and he would have at least six kids all piled on top of him laughing and having fun—and probably fulfilling some lost dreams for the children. It was then that I knew this must be the right one.

Guess what?

God's plan for my life was better than mine. Who knew? Steve is the most amazing God-loving husband and father I could ever ask for. He was immediately given the gift of my crazy, big family. Through both of our life experiences, we have lived with intention regarding the priorities in our family. Our marriage comes before our kids. We believe that this is the best gift we can give our four children. We want them to understand that life is not *"all about them,"* and we try to demonstrate that through everyday life. They never know who will be living with us for a while, or what project they will be working on with us because we want them to truly make a difference in society. We believe that each one has a specific purpose in life and it is their mission to accomplish it. We laugh really hard, and we work really hard as a family, and I am sure God intervened way back then.

Heather, Director of Pink Ribbon Girls

Dayton, Ohio

We Have Become Stronger, The Three Of Us

I had the good life. I was living the dream. My husband and I married young. Out of four children we were blessed to raise two because both of our boys died at birth due to similar genetic complications. Both of the girls are beautiful and healthy teenage young ladies. We had the perfect family. And then life changed. My husband died, and I was now a single mom. Not a life that anyone ever dreams - a widowed single mom. A mother, who literally, without a moment's notice, had to think about the unthinkable, and imagine the unimaginable.

Allen and I were always there for each other. We were each other's best friends. He was our family protector. It has taken me years to somehow lessen the pain. Time truly does heal, but death leaves such a large emptiness in our hearts that it takes years to heal. For days, weeks, even months after the death of my husband I spent most of those hours mourning, sad, and alone. Unsure of what my future would hold, unsure of whom I was going to be. It wasn't until I looked in my daughters' eyes and saw the same pain that I knew I needed to move forward, because in addition to the pain, they were looking for guidance.

What do we do from here? Who will protect us now? Is there life after loss? I knew from that moment that I had to step up my game. I had to be the mom and the dad. I was totally responsible for my daughters and keeping the memory of Allen alive. We miss how things used to be, and it's hard not to think of how things should have been, but life is good.

We moved from the home we had made in New Orleans, back to my home state of Ohio. This proved to be a painful but necessary move to be closer to family. We make a yearly trip back to New Orleans to visit friends, and oftentimes throughout the year visit my husbands' family in Texas. My girls are happy, and that is what makes me happy. We have continued several traditions, like in the weeks leading up to Mardi Gras we order a King Cake to be delivered from one of the best bakeries in New Orleans. We share recipes with our friends still in New Orleans so that we can connect through friends and food.

We confide in each other and rely on each other. We have become stronger, the three of us. We lean on each other and share opinions, thoughts, and give encouragement and compassion. We are making our own memories all the while reminiscing about old ones. In everything we do, we do it with love. It feels so good to laugh, not just smile or chuckle—but a honest-to-goodness laugh, and we have many of those.

Susan, Accountant Specialist, Plain City, Ohio

The Greatest Gift My Daddy Ever Gave Me

If I had to choose only one word to describe my daddy I wouldn't know which one of many to choose - but if I must, I pick MINE.

Growing up I always knew that come five thirty every evening that the table had to be set when daddy walked in the door. The next thirty minutes was our "play time" with him where he would tickle us, chase us, or help us with homework - whatever the need until it was time for dinner.

As we got older and we became more involved with sports, friends and school - our nightly dinners telling about our day and our *"daddy"* time got shorter and shorter. We would call him at work at times and ask what time he would be home or what he was doing - he would always reply 'making money to buy some hamburgers'. He was making sure he was providing the best life for his family, following in my 'pop pops' footsteps and how he was raised.

Summers were always hard. Our routines were changing and we always wanted to go here and there and everywhere, as we got older. I spent my summers swimming for our local swim club. I hated having to get up early because I was on summer break but as daddy always said, *'You made the commitment and you have to stick with it!'* My swim meets were all over the Dayton area and while dad was always working he always timed it just right to see me swim, cheer me on and give some wisdom for the next meet. It's like he had super powers of knowing just what to say and where I needed him to be.

I recently purchased my first home, scared to death and not knowing a lot about home rehab I called my dad with tears streaming down my face. I was overwhelmed by the daunting task and couldn't see the end in sight. I knew all the improvements I wanted and I knew two things; he is a general contractor and I am his daughter! And so the work began. Every weekend for what seems like forever – with my mom, sisters, brother-in-laws and myself, his goal was to make this house into my home and teaching everything he could along the way.

Since finishing the home I have filled his "off time" with my crazy ideas; new paver patio, refinishing the basement, glass block windows, teaching me how to golf, taking me to the shooting range, or meeting me for a snack and drink at the local watering hole. These are all the moments I wish I had more of. The greatest gift he has ever given me is his time.

Ellen the Entrepreneur, Tipp City

CHAPTER FOUR

THE CAREER BALLOON

I wondered for a while if I was qualified to write this chapter about the career balloon at age sixty-six. It seems that retirement age in America continues to change on a regular basis, and I continue not to be concerned by the topic. When people ask me why I have not retired or why I am not planning on retiring very soon, my response is simple. *"My definition of retirement means that you quit your job and I have yet to have a job,"* and, thus, I do not feel that I qualify to retire by my own standard.

The dictionary definition of a *job* is: *A piece of work, a specific task done as part of a routine, anything a person is expected or obliged to do*. And since the *"jobs"* that I have had in my life for the most part do not fit the definition, how then do I retire from something that I have yet to begin?

Never Take My Career Or Myself Too Seriously

The amazing part of my life has been that I can pinpoint the exact day of my teenage life when I made the decision that *"I would never take my career or myself too seriously."* I realized in 1965 where my career would fit into the rest of my life.

I am truly blessed that I can count the days in my life that I have not been excited to get up in the morning and go to *"work."* As a teacher, coach, youth pastor, entrepreneur, social entrepreneur and all the other roles that I have had, I never saw them as *a specific task to be done or a routine that I was in*. My career has always felt more like something that would be part of my hobby balloon rather than my career balloon. The times I have changed careers seemed to have come about quickly. I can count the days I did not like my career. When it came to a point of feeling like a *"job,"* I knew it was time to seek out something that would again more seem more like a hobby than a real job.

My thinking changed forever when I was a senior in high school because of my dad. He had worked for American Telephone and Telegraph (AT&T) most of his career. Unlike today, when researchers say that the average person will probably have more than seven jobs, in my dad's generation it was more like one or two. I cannot remember a day as I was growing up that he did not put on his white shirt and bow tie, eat his hardboiled egg and a piece of toast for breakfast, and head out the door for his 45-minute drive to work. He never missed a day. He was never late. And he never left work early.

What was his job? He said he was never allowed to tell us what kind of work he did, so even today I have no clue. He said it was *"classified and top secret,"* and I had no idea what that meant—but I was proud of him because at that time Russia was on our minds a lot in America, and I thought somehow he was protecting us from something.

With all of his faithfulness to his job, it all ended in just one day. He returned home one day from work, and at dinner he announced that he had been laid off. The government's defense budget had been cut, and they told him that there was no need for him to think about ever returning. Being 17 years old, I really did not know what all that meant, but I do remember being very angry and sad. I wasn't mad at him, and not sure that I was mad that he lost his income, but I could not understand how they could ever do that to someone who never missed a day of work in his life—never late—and was so committed to whatever his drawing and blueprints were that he brought them home and worked on them every night.

We Never Talked About His Losing The Job

I never really knew what to say, and I don't think he did either. It was really the only job I can remember he ever had while I was growing up. Looking back, I think he was dealing with two issues. The first was the idea of losing his income—but also he had the fear of what he would do next. I am not sure that there were not jobs to be had, but I know he lacked the confidence that he could do anything else. As he would say, *"At my age no one wants to train me."* This became somewhat of a self-fulfilling prophecy.

In the spring and summer of my senior year, I had a really good job, building in-ground swimming pools for one of the coaches at school. We were expected to work really hard, and we did. We were paid based on our output and how many pools we could put in each week. He was a great motivator, and for teenaged me that translated into a very high-paying, fun and challenging job.

One day I happened to see one of my dad's paychecks from his new *"career,"* which he explained as *"until something better comes along."* Looking at his paycheck on the kitchen counter was a moment I will remember forever. I realized that at age seventeen I was earning a lot more money than he was. He never knew that I saw his check, but it continued to fuel my anger. We were not poor, we were not hungry, but I continued to feel so bad for him because I knew how hard he had worked for our family his entire life. That incident seemed to fester in my thinking for some time, and at some point I told myself, *"That will never happen to me."* It is one of those decisions in life that shifts something inside of you, becoming part of your DNA, but you can't see its importance at the moment.

My Dad's Loss Became My Gain

What was I thinking when I made a decision like that? What did I know about the world of work? What skills did I have? What financial responsibilities did I really have? For weeks I could not imagine that life could be so unfair, and yet there was nothing he or I could do about it. He was willing to be retrained, travel wherever he needed to and do whatever was needed. I think because of the culture, his age and his mindset, and the idea that he thought had he had failed, he lost his identity and never recovered. The jobs ahead of him were more menial in nature— some were jobs that people gave him as a favor until *"things get better."* But they never did, and he just waited for retirement to come.

What impact would this have on my life? I know now that it was one of the most important life lessons for me. By this time I had had lots of jobs as a kid and had a great work ethic. I didn't have a desire to get rich; I think I just liked the challenge of having a job, making money and providing for myself. My teenage years were consumed with lawn mowing, a paper route, snow shoveling, door-to-door sales, working as a stock boy and even one summer riding around on a vegetable truck and selling fruit and vegetables door-to-door. I made one dollar an hour, riding that truck five days a week, and on Friday afternoon, bringing home my fifteen dollars plus some tip money, fulfilled my every dream!

Having had the opportunity to talk with so many fathers of teens, they would agree that their Career Balloon was their biggest and the focus of their lives. They explained that the Career Balloon was what enabled the Financial Balloon. The Financial Balloon was what provided for the Family Balloon. Yet other balloons were small because of the lack of time after a sixty-hour workweek, and they lacked time to even create the vision. What they didn't understand from the viewpoint of their children was that money was not the issue they cared about—they cared about having time with their dad, and a dad that would care more about them than his career.

Through all those conversations I am always reminded how thankful I am for the decision that I made as a teen. By not worrying about having this great big career balloon, I made it a priority every day to work just as hard on the other nine balloons.

I always love talking with teens about their mothers' balloons and how they see them in comparison to their dads'. With most moms now in the workforce it is always interesting that teens don't see Mom as having this giant career balloon. Even though moms have a full-time career just like dads, teens will instantly say, *"She can't have a giant career because she has to take care of all the other stuff in our family."* These statements make me change the direction of the conversation quickly as I sure don't want to get involved in family arguments!

When I coach parents in implementing the Ten Balloons, I ask them to think how they believe their children perceive them, and then help them decide whether it is true of false. I think our legacies are built on our balloons. I am always more concerned with what values and traditions parents instill in their children as compared to how hard they worked and how dedicated they are to something that might just change in an instant.

When I talk to people about my career mission statement, I am always cautious in how I approach the topic. First, I remind them that each person must determine their own mission and not be influenced by others' ideas or opinions. It did not take me long to figure out mine.

Hey Shoeshine Boy!

My hope for teens today is that their career balloon has already started by the time I meet them. I usually begin sessions with the assignment of *"List the jobs you have had so far in life."* Instantly, you see a microcosmic view of our culture. Some kids have been protected from ever having any responsibility by their parents. Some are too busy with video games for a job. Some are very lazy. And some are soaring, based on their parents' expectations for them.

Some already have an entrepreneurial mindset. Although I never knew the word *entrepreneur* as a kid, I was one. I thrived on taking risks, and risk-taking was what enabled me to have my earliest jobs. One of the funniest was when I was 11 years old in Parsippany, New Jersey. Out of nowhere I decided one day that I could make a lot of money shining shoes. I went to the basement, found some wood, and designed and created a very primitive-looking shoeshine box. I loaded it with borrowed supplies from my father.

The only problem with this idea is that we lived a block from a lake, and there was little opportunity to find shoes to shine. Discussing my dilemma with my uncle Vic, he offered to take me to the local tavern one day after his workday. It is hard to describe the tavern in detail, but it had about 15 stools at the bar and a shuffleboard game that ran the length of the bar, and not much else. On any given afternoon there were probably five to eight *"regulars"* who would drop in for a beer or two before heading home.

I am sure my uncle is responsible for making my shoeshine business a success by encouraging his friends to help out his *"entrepreneurial nephew"* with a ten-cent shoeshine! I was not very good at shining shoes my first day—but no one seemed to care. They were way more interested in teaching me how to shine shoes and how to work than how their shoes turned out. Uncle Vic invited me to join him on a regular basis after that. I remember walking home when finished and thinking I was one of the richest kids in the world, with fifty-sixty cents in my pocket.

Each of us can name important people in our lives who helped form our values and some of our strengths. My high school cross-country coach, Ed Mathers, is probably the person in my life to whom I owe the most for helping me determine my future and its success. I went out for the team with little idea of what the sport was about and no personal history in running. The short story of my four years is that I succeeded more than I ever imagined. Being on the varsity team and co-captain of the team for a season was something I was very proud of. Although I knew the Olympics were not in my future, I did realize that I wanted to coach because I knew what an impact it had on my life, and I thought how much fun that would be in my future.

Mr. Staninas was my mechanical drawing teacher. He influenced me in similar ways and helped me realize that being a shop teacher (called vocational education today) would encompass all of my passions. He also told me I could be an athletic coach while being a teacher. Their influence set my career balloon direction for life.

My Father-in-Law Fred

After nine years in the school system I decided that I had accomplished all I wanted in teaching and coaching so I quit. My father-in-law decided we needed to have our first ever heart-to-heart conversation. *"How can you throw away your college degree just like that?"* I was somewhat taken aback by what he said because I never saw it that way. I loved teaching and I loved coaching. I just wanted a change of venue. I knew that I had lost some of my passion for teaching—but not coaching—and I knew in my heart that it was not really right to just continuing teaching because at that time it opened the door to coaching. He, like my dad, had a really different concept of working. After our conversation, he still didn't really understand my motive. But then again, in his eyes my job was his daughter's security—and he was being a great father, just trying to protect his daughter. In his mind he was trying to stop me from making a mistake that I might later regret.

If Fred was still alive, I would like to remind him that forty-five years later I am still teaching and coaching. The venues are different—the audience changes—but the passion I had at 14 years old still continues today.

Words To Parents And Grandparents

How does one begin helping others in search of a career balloon? I love doing workshops with students about careers. I ask them what they want to do in the future. Most look at me like I am from another planet. *"Why would we care about that now? We have lots of time before we need to make that decision."* Aren't these the same students whose parents have them on every school sport team, traveling teams and community teams? How many are thinking about what college they want to play for? How many are thinking professional sports? And yet the parents say, *"They have lots of time to figure their future out,"* as they drive the children to yet another practice.

My *Ten Balloons* session begins with this: *"Write down three things that you love to do."* It can't be three sports, only one, and what else besides sports? *"Let's pretend now that you are twenty-two years old, and I can hand a you a college degree in any of those areas that you wrote down—and you can start working tomorrow. What would your list look like now?"*

One of the weaknesses of growing up in America today is the lack of dreaming. Children and teens are programmed in everything from the earliest age. In discussing this topic with my wife as she was teaching kindergarten, she explained that some students entering her class had already lost some of their creativity and their ability to dream.

The next thing I have them do is write about why they would really like one of their options as a job, and I ask them to write five reasons why. We talk about them and also the obstacles they see in getting that job. The majority of the answers have come from their parents: *"You won't make enough money in that career...your grades are not good enough...we can't afford to send you to school that long."*

Imagine a world where parents and grandparents would take time to talk about careers. Maybe take them on business and factory tours, and, most importantly, on a visit to their workplace. Some may start a business together, and others might just have continual conversations about the world of work and how they see themselves fitting in.

Parents sit for hours watching practices and rehearsals. They would never think about missing a game or event all season—and travel to the ends of the earth to support their kids in every type of school activity. Yet many, both parents and grandparents, often miss the opportunity to share their knowledge, wisdom and encouragement as it relates to careers.

An Interview:

The Youthful Pursuit Of A Magic Career

As a freshman in high school I understand that you don't consider *Tyler the Magician* a business—even though you have a business name, logo and business cards; you continually develop your product; you make money and continue to have a plan to expand the scope and depth of your non-business—what am I missing here? I would call that an amazing business.

Do you mind if I ask you a few questions?

When did your "non-business" begin? This dream has been developing since I was in third grade, and yes, I am still developing it today. The idea actually started because I wanted to become a cartoonist because I liked the idea of making people happy. I developed my own character (Jim) and involved him in what I thought were funny situations. Around that age I discovered magic and realized that I could convey my message through it instead.

What do you mean you discovered magic? On Christmas Day of 2009 my mother gave me a magic kit. I later discovered books and tricks that belonged to her father. I studied the art day and night—eventually evolving it into a show that I have performed all across the country.

What were some early lessons that you learned about your "non-business"? I have learned and relearned many times that I should not worry about making money. For me, it's a difficult lesson because the world is scary—it wants you to play the *"greed game"*—making money the focus of everything. I am learning that the reality is exactly the opposite. Money is just the byproduct of having a quality product and enjoying what I do.

What is the scope of your business? As the name *Tyler Does Magic* implies, I do magic. My audiences range from children's birthday parties to corporate events and everything in between—from audiences of two to 1200 people. I have perform anywhere from church basements to some of the most beautiful theaters in America.

Where have your performances taken you? I've performed in Las Vegas, Virginia, New Jersey, New York City, Dallas and many other cool places!

At times do you see Tyler Does Magic as your hobby balloon? Interestingly enough, yes, I do. I have been competing in magic competitions for years where the goal has primarily been to gain excellence. I enjoy learning from, and being challenged by, my peers as well as the veteran magicians who enjoy a mentoring relationship with some of us younger magicians.

So if you do compete, how have you done? Well, since you asked, I received First Place in a National Competition held in Columbus, Ohio, and was ranked second in the world as a magician under the age of 17 in 2011.

Where do you see Tyler Does Magic heading through your high school years? As a freshman, I am redeveloping my product for the real world. During my sophomore year I plan on performing on a more consistent basis and upping my professionalism. From there, the sky's the limit.

Why do you think your strengths are for making this happen? I love what I do, and I am just young enough to believe that anything is possible. Second, I have spent a lot of time performing and being onstage, which allows me develop my performance in ways practice never could.

What are some of the most satisfying things of owning your own business? I believe in what I do. I love it. When I see that I have captured the audience's attention, I feel successful. My hope when working with children and my peers is that I can inspire them to dream great dreams also.

Do you foresee this turning into your career later in life? Absolutely! I will continue to develop my product constantly, and I have every intention to pursue it as my profession.

Tyler The Magician, Van Wert, Ohio

Judge Cathy's Thirteen-Year-Old Self

I knew the summer before I started high school that I wanted to be a lawyer, a departure from the norm in my family comprised of doctors and contractors. Male doctors and contractors at that; no female in my family had ever pursued a career.

Nonetheless, off I went to undergraduate and law school, never wavering from the fact I was going to be a lawyer. Of course, I didn't really know what kind of lawyer I would be, but I was pretty confident that I would be a research geek, toiling away for hours in dusty old law books. Funny how life changes!

Two years out of law school, I found myself with my own law practice, going to court and defending juveniles. And I discovered I loved that part of the law: the intricacies of keeping families together and rehabilitating young criminals in the hopes they could stay out of prison. Juvenile law became my passion; I soon became an assistant district attorney with my sole focus on juvenile crime. In 2000, the state created a new position for our circuit: Juvenile Court Referee, presiding over the juvenile cases filed in our county. And I was hired for that position.

Much like my decision to be a lawyer, I didn't have a role model to follow in this new position. So, as with all other of my career decisions, I blazed ahead and hoped for the best. And the best it has been. I love my job even though days can be very frustrating and, at times, heartbreaking. But those days when a family is reunited or when a child finds sobriety and enters college make all the frustration and heartbreak worthwhile. I often have to get in the trenches with these families or try to outsmart a teenager. And the answers I find aren't answers that can be found in a dusty old law book.

I am a lawyer and a judge. I make a difference. And I am good at it. My thirteen-year-old self sometimes can't believe how lucky I am to have made this life.

Judge Cathy, Huntsville, Alabama

CHAPTER FIVE

THE MENTAL BALLOON

My school grades were always a source of conversation in my family growing up. I remember on many nights going to bed and awaiting my parent's return from their annual parent-teacher meeting. They would come into my room following their conference to discuss the latest findings of the semester. Somehow they forgot that the message given on these evenings was not a new one for me. The conversation usually include some version of *"Listen to us when we are talking to you!"* and *"Your teacher said that you are not working up to your potential!"* To those comments I learned it was best not to offer any kind of rebuttal and instead just let them rant. It wasn't like my report card was plagued with D's and F's, it was just that I was not receiving the consistent A's and B's that my parents were probably wishing I had. I had concluded long before the evening sermon that I would not give them my view on my academic progress, as I knew it probably would not have been well received. Telling your parents that you are trying your hardest is not a good defense, and the reality was that I was not going to be a straight-A student, no matter how hard I tried.

The Quality Of Output Is Determined By The Quality Of The Input

The concept behind the mental balloon is focused on the things you put into your brain that are not required to be there by some third-party authority. The idea of information not being required comes from the notion that although high school and college reading is important, more often than not it is only just part of an academic benchmark.

Most of my mental balloon as a child was made up of a very small amount of television, taken in through our thirteen-inch, black-and-white set that offered three New York City channels. TV had not yet become an American value, and I was very content creating my own fun either inside or outdoors.

Some of my other input included my purchasing of comic books at the local grocery store. It was a weekly Saturday tradition, where I would sit on the floor and read while my mother shopped. I selected my favorite two each week to take home to build to my collection. In time not only would I read the comics from cover to cover, but I also began drawing the characters into a sketchpad, which helped fuel my passion for sketching and drawing.

Growing up, we received the newspaper each afternoon in our home. I always thought it was my responsibility to read the comics, and, on occasion, to check out the sports section. Beyond that, I felt the newspaper was written for my parents, but never for me.

In Seven Minutes The Way I Thought About Education Changed

It was the last few days of high school, and my final grade from my English teacher came early. In those days students took their report card to each teacher to receive comments and grades.

Being enrolled in this English class had always seemed like some sort of conspiracy against me. Regardless of the effort I put into the assignments, the gap between my effort and my teacher's expectations for the class seemed to grow exponentially. After all these years I now have my own explanation of how this conspiracy theory began. My mother must have sneaked into school one day, knowing all about my slow progress in the English language. In a last ditch effort to salvage my education she had the school transfer me into a class with all the *"smarter students."* In today's world that would be called Honors English or some other fancy title that made me feel isolated from the rest of the world.

Looking around the room, I realized that I had never been in class with a majority of these students in my four years at Parsippany High School, thus solidifying my belief in the conspiracy theory. These students were probably going to be ranked at the top of the class; two would be our valedictorian and salutatorian, and then there was me.

The other great reason for my theory is that with every paper I turned in, Mr. Perlett seemed to return the paper with more of his black ink on it than mine. He would fill the margins with his ideas, suggestions and, most importantly, his encouragement for me to keep on trying. He would often mention how he liked my creative ideas in response to the reading and his questions—yet he knew I struggled with using the proper grammar and sentence structure. To this day I smile and can only imagine the battle my parents waged to get me into this class.

Did Enduring The Difficulty Of Being In This Class Work?

When I went forward to his desk to get my grade, I was not very excited. As he entered the grade, I could see from over his shoulder that it was a C, and I was remarkably surprised. I knew that my collection of D's and F's on my papers all semester did not average out to a C. But what student would ever be so stupid to question a teacher about that decision? Following his mark, I opened my mouth to ask, *"Mr. Perlett, I'm just wondering how I got such a high grade. Are you sure you don't have me confused with someone else?"* He responded with, *"I don't make mistakes in grading. If you want to keep that grade, come and see me today after school."*

> *"Mike, I know you worked harder than just about any student in my class. You turned in every assignment, and it seemed like you were determined to succeed. I like you—I think you have some great potential, and I want to give you some advice that someone once gave me. Have a seat here by my desk."*

Now I was scared. Can't I just take the grade card, the compliments and run? Graduation is a few days away, and you just gave me the best present ever! I pulled up a chair close to his desk, per his suggestion, and he reached in the trashcan and pulled out the morning paper. *"Read this much? Let me guess, the sports and the comics?"* To which I responded in the affirmative, but wondered how he could be so smart.

"Mike, I want to give you some advice and an idea that will raise your college grades by a whole letter." He told me to follow his finger as he read simply the headlines and captions under each picture in the paper. *"You know Mike, if you do what I say it will take you less ten minutes a day to do this."* And so, I followed his finger—he paused at times, but never made a comment about anything he read.

When he finished, he folded up the paper and set it back in the trashcan. *"If I gave that paper back to you, do you think that there were two or three stories that you would like to read more about?"* My answer was an instant yes. He got my attention in a way that he had hoped for, and I saw how much I was missing in the newspaper. My interest was piqued from some of the catchy titles and, of course, the pictures, which visually hooked me into wanting to know more of the details.

I was seventeen on the day of our meeting. I am not sure exactly what I was feeling except excitement about being allowed to keep my C. After being in his class all year, it seemed strange to me that in less than ten minutes he had impacted my life more than he did all year. Looking back, I see how effective he was as a teacher. All year I did my assignments because he made class interesting, and I wanted to read the stories and learn the meaning of them. Where I struggled was being able to communicate effectively in writing at the level he expected. I wonder if it was the investment he made in me throughout the year by taking time to diligently grade my papers that motivated him to take the time after school with me, again ensuring the payoff in his yearlong investment in my future.

I then graduated from high school, and went off to college. About a month into my freshman year at Eastern Kentucky University, I had one of those *"Aha!"* moments of life. The *Louisville Courier Journal* was offering a free month-long subscription to college students, and since it was free, I asked myself, *"Why not?"* The *"aha!"* came as I was sitting on my bed reading the paper and had lost track of time as I scanned the headlines. I was reading for an hour and did a quick reality check with myself: *"What in the world are you doing reading for an hour?"*

That day after school with Mr. Perlett changed my life forever. In the fifty years since then I can probably count the days that I have not read the newspaper, and read it in the way that he taught. Most days, I read two newspapers and have developed a love for magazines and books.

Every day I learn something new, some good and also some bad. I learn more about places I have been—and see places I would like to visit. I see problems in the world and wonder if I could be part of the solution.

I have found that a half-hour television news show has about fourteen minutes of news—and much of that is reported over and over. I love the newspaper because if I am not interested in the title of the article I go to the next one; it is such an efficient way of gathering information and learning. Mr. Perlett never realized that he changed my destiny and the destiny of the hundreds in my workshops who adopted his simple idea and made it work.

Looking Back—And Looking Forward

I think that the idea of input will always be in flux. As you go through life stages, you might have more or less time to invest in your own interests. You may also find the need and desire to learn more about different areas. I am for thankful my high school days, where I began to understand what my purpose statement would be in the area of mental, *Looking back and looking forward,* and that reading is what has helped me define my life.

I recently received an email from Elizabeth, a long-time friend, after a conversation we were having about some new dreams, goals and adventures in the upcoming year. I was intrigued when she wrote about her plan for the New Year that she has labeled one—one—one. And so I asked her to tell me more about what that meant.

One. One. One.

As a mom, a professor and a minister, it is incredibly easy to feel like a prisoner of my to-do list. There are emails to be sent, doctors' appointments to make, papers to grade, and sermons to write. The list is never completed—our world is always asking more of us.

Over the years, I've found that I get a great sense of accomplishment when I am able to cross something off my list. We live in a culture that tells us to be busy and to be efficient. It is almost as if we think we become better people when we manage our list of tasks better. But often, getting through the day can sum up the long-term vision for the life we want to live.

The writer Annie Dillard reminds us *"how we spend our days is how we spend our lives."* I saw this quote on a church sign in 2003, and it was like a punch in the stomach. My life was a series of sending emails, doing dishes, writing papers (I was a seminary student at the time), going to sleep, and waking up, only to start all over again. It is a pattern I have struggled with for years.

This year, over a decade after I first read the quote, I am still struggling with how I spend my days. As one way to move closer to the life I want—a life that is not defined by my to-do list—I have, with some success, committed to a one–one–one plan. One hour of reading a day. One hour of writing a day. One hour of exercise/physical activity a day. I am lucky that I am able to make plenty of time to spend with my son, but the reading-writing-exercise trio often feels easy for me to put off. For me, these are slow things— they cannot be done quickly or easily, and the payoff doesn't come in one day. The hope is that I can carve out three hours of my day that moves me closer to living the life that I want—a richer life of health, reflection and learning—that pushes back on our to-do-list culture.

Elizabeth, Assistant Professor, Honors College, Western Kentucky University

I appreciate the honesty of Elizabeth in her journey. I met her when she was a teenager, and she has always been one of those people who have had a great impact on my life because of her continual pursuit of knowledge. Her school and career journey have been fun to watch and be a part of as she has a mindset to continually improve in all areas of her life.

The Value of a Journal

One advantage in keeping a journal is that you become aware with reassuring clarity of the changes which you constantly suffer and which, in a general way, are naturally believed, surmised and admitted by you, but which you'll unconsciously deny when it comes to the point of gaining hope or peace from such an admission.

In the journal you find proof that in situations which today would seem unbearable, you lived, looked around and wrote down observations, that this right hand moved then as it does today, when we may be wiser because we are able to look back upon our former condition, and for that very reason have got to admit the courage of our earlier striving in which we persisted even in sheer ignorance.

Franz Kafka, 20th century German novelist

I wish I could have met Franz Kafka when I first undertook the idea of journaling. My introduction to writing my thoughts down came through the church, when it was explained how important it could be in your faith journey. The problem was that I seemed to do it only when I was in a particular situation. At retreats and camps there always seemed to be a portion of the time set aside for practicing the art of journaling, and these proved to be journal-writing-inducing environments.

I returned home from these times understanding some of the benefits of this new discipline, yet my commitment was short-lived and it seemed like a duty more than a new way for me to learn about myself and the world around me.

I wish that I had also learned sooner what I absorbed as a result of listening to one high school student. Years after the Columbine shooting in Colorado, a sister of one of the students went on a nationwide tour to tell the story about her sister and some of the other victims. As part of her presentation she held up a journal and read some of the thoughts from her sister's writings in the weeks before she was murdered. The interesting part for me was how she explained the importance of the journals to her life now, in memory of her sister. Her words became a powerful awakening for me. She explained how her sister's journaling was very random— and she was now following in her path. She explained how journaling for her was a way to process her own life when she didn't want to talk to anyone else, because at times she felt no one could ever understand her situation. She reassured the listeners that the benefit of journaling for her came not in the frequency, but in the occasion. It was a source of fulfillment in her life.

This became one of those *"wow"* moments for me, and a pivotal part of how I could process my life in a new way. My frustration at that time with journaling was that I thought it had to be a daily habit. I was not thrilled at the idea of starting and stopping until it became an ingrained and forced habit. Since hearing about this young lady's story, journaling has been probably what has brought the most sanity to my life.

Journaling for me can take on many forms. Sometimes it can almost be like a travelogue, and a log of the day's adventures. Other times it is more of a pep talk to myself when things seem out of control or headed for disaster. One of my favorites ways to journal is with a two-part assignment that I give myself. The first is to write the top thirty or so things in my life from that week. It can be about my career, family, adventure (I go through the balloons), and on most days it is an easy task. And then, because the reason I usually do this is because of my frustration about something or someone, my task is to write down the top three things that I am struggling with at that time. Ironically, because of the positive list that sits in front of me, the negatives often seem so useless to write about. But I do write down the three, and if I can come up with more, I write them down also. Time after time, I end my time of journaling feeling like a cured man. The burdens do not go away, but instead are put into perspective.

Got God?

Not too long ago, I made a decision to write at least half of my journal entries based on Scripture. I find that I get bored doing the same thing day after day, and I realized that Scriptures come my way often through sermons, conversations and sometimes by just opening the Bible randomly. What I have found is that in most cases the Scripture identified that day was the perfect match to where I am at the time in my life. I like to read the Scripture, always asking the same question, *"Does this apply to me today?"* and if so, *"How?"* I may spend a day or two going back to it, reading verses before or after it, and having my own Bible study. I find that so often what I learn through the Scripture is something I think others in my sphere of influence would be interested in also, and so I send them a quick email. My writing is random. If I miss a day, miss a week, it's not like I feel I missed anything. I write not based on habit, but by need or opportunity.

The funniest (and yet saddest) story I have about journaling comes from when I was the youth pastor. One of the *"spiritual leaders"* of the church came into my office to talk about how strong her faith was, and how she thought that I needed some advice on how to improve my life as a Christian. She went on to explain how she and her husband would arise at 5:00 a.m. every day and read the Scriptures together. They would then journal and pray together. She was extremely adamant that it was the best idea ever, and that Sherri and I should do that because of my role with the young people in the church. She believed that I needed to model daily

Christian disciplines to them.

I smiled as she left my office, graciously thanking her for her time and for being so concerned about our youth ministry and me, though that was one the biggest lies I have ever told. In my mind I was really thanking her for getting out of my office. I instantly had a rebuttal in mind, but knew that would have gotten out instantly in how I was *"so not teachable."* So I thought it best to have the conversation with myself.

> *Dear Ms. Spiritual Church Lady,*
>
> *If I did wake my wife up at 5:00 a.m. every morning, the marriage might soon be over.*
>
> *Coincidently, I do get up every morning at 5:00 a.m., but instead of annoying Sherri I head to McDonald's for a cup of coffee, a free newspaper and a time of not talking to anyone.*
>
> *We have already tried having Bible study together, and it did not work. I realized from hearing other "super-Christians" like yourself that I would probably not make it into heaven because of not having this type of daily devotional schedule. I decided that I would take the risk of going to Hell and explain my reasons to God instead of a "church lady" like you.*
>
> *If I want ideas from you in the future, I will come to your office and ask you. And by the way, why don't you please stop wasting your time judging me?*

I never told her my thoughts—it just was not the needed thing to do.

As with all the balloons, deciding what is important for you and what works for you is the most important thing that any of us can ever do. Don't compare your balloons with others'—but instead just be able to answer the questions about what will make up each of the balloons in your life.

Good News. Bad News.

One of the best pieces of advice I ever received in life came from a man who struggled with reading the Bible on a regular basis. He told me that the turning point in his life came when he realized that although reading the Bible every day was following what he was taught to do, he didn't think it was making him a much better person. He spoke boldly about the day he started reading the newspaper every day, and the Bible, too. His smile, his confidence and his determination showed when he said, *"I now live my life knowing that the newspaper on most days tells of the 'bad news' within our communities, America and the world. The life change for me was realizing that the Bible and 'good news' came to make more sense to help me in discerning what needs in the world I might be able to help with."*

I like the decisions that I have made about my mental balloon. I have hunger and passion to continue to learn. When I think about how I like to learn, I realize that my choices would not work for the majority of people. That is the beauty of the balloons and being able to wrestle with each one. Out of all of the balloons, I think the mental balloon poses one of the best questions for us. What do you put into your brain on a regular basis? The idea that there is a direct correlation between your input, what you put into your brain, and your output, how you live your life each day, is one worth consideration.

Yes, I am a Rocket Scientist

In thinking about my mental balloon, I was challenged to think back in my life and wonder why—why have I always had a quest for knowledge? Throughout my life, I have constantly challenged myself to gather in a wealth of information found in books, newspaper articles, magazines, radio, television, the Internet and all other media. I enjoy challenging speakers, lectures, rigorous discussions and interaction with others.

I am a husband, father, grandfather, and yes, I am a rocket scientist—a.k.a. an aerospace engineer. One might believe all the stars were aligned and my life was on a predetermined path, but I would argue I am more a creation of a rich educational environment, driving me into the realm of science and engineering. I must acknowledge three men's influence in my life.

Grandpa Lynch was in WWI with the first Aero Squadron, where as a mechanic in France he maintained some of the earliest aircraft in history. With his highly inquisitive mind and an active sense of humor he loved baseball, read current events, told stories in competitions, and was a family historian. Grandpa encouraged me as a young boy when I became interested in airplanes, rockets and other assorted science- and technology-related hobbies.

I never knew Grandpa Copeland, but his love of education and reasoned thought came through my mom to me. He studied in Colorado and California. He survived the great depression in Oklahoma, teaching high school math and science as well as farming. His disciplined approach to knowledge was passed on to me with mom's gentle encouragement.

My father, Homer, loved God, life and people, and studied rural sociology before attending seminary and serving as a pastor for 40 years. Late in life, dad suffered a major stroke. He lost the use of his right side and most motor skills required to speak and communicate clearly. But for nearly seven years he pushed on. With a strong mind trapped in a broken body, Dad was able to reinvent his communication pathways each day.

And so the quest continues. Now having four daughters, I am so proud of each of their successes and how I see in them their pursuit of knowledge and education—continuing the family legacy. I am blessed.

Lin, the father and grandfather of many, Urbana, Ohio

CHAPTER SIX THE EPIDEMIC OF BEING BUSY

The entire point of having a mental balloon stems from the idea that our mental state of mind can affect the other areas of our lives. I consider myself blessed to have gone to a leadership conference in the early '80s, where I listened to Gordon MacDonald speaking on the topic of his book, *ordering Your Private World.* It was one of those times of teaching when I was able to glean a few principles and return home and implement them immediately. To this day I hold dearly the decisions I made that day.

> In today's world if you are not busy
> all the time then you appear to
> some to be less of a person.

I have a list of seven qualities that I teach high school students and I ensure them that these qualities, if they embrace them, will set them up for a lifetime of success. I begin the list with *"Do not think of yourself more highly than you ought"* (Romans 12:3).

"Being busy" is an epidemic. When I talk with people who may want me to be involved in something, they usually follow their question with their own answer, *"Oh, you are probably way too busy."* To which I answer, *"No, not really, I am really not that busy most days and weeks."* The conversation then goes on so they can tell me about how busy they are—very busy telling me how important they are. I made a decision twenty-five years ago that *"being busy"* was not how I wanted to define—or live—my life.

With students, *"being busy and being important"* means that they must be in advanced classes, in multiple sports and in numerous school activities to help ensure that they can keep their parents busy also. I have watched the results of so many young people who were *"so busy"* in sports at an early age that they soon tire, quit, and then *"got busy,"* taking up something new to fill that void in their life created by free time. Unfortunately, we see so many unhappy young people in spite of the fact that they are busy all the time. The belief that we help our children's self-esteem and image backfires for many.

What did Gordon teach in that conference that changed my thinking forever? He spoke about how to have a balanced day, a balanced week, and eventually, a balanced month and year. Recognizing that we all have many responsibilities in life, his solution is based on the idea that we schedule at least a third of every day where we are not busy. Most people, when hearing that idea, respond that it is impossible.

We live in a world where people are proud of their giant *"to-do"* lists each day. I hear it so often from retired friends, "I am busier now that ever before," which makes me question my own self-esteem: *"Should I be doing more with my life?"*

The Assignment Is Simple

Make your own calendar and divide each day into three sections. You determine what a morning session might look like. If you are an early riser, it might be 5:00 a.m. to noon. The second could be noon to dinnertime, and the last would be your evening. There are no guidelines that they be equal or how long. The goal is to initially block out one section each day where you are not busy. (Sleep does not count.) Eventually you don't need to do this on paper, as it becomes a lifestyle. It becomes refreshing knowing that you have time for yourself, and an attitude that reflects that you are ready for the rest of the day.

For me, it became a weekly discipline to look at my week each Sunday morning and make a schedule of all the time that I would not be busy. Some days, it would be morning, some, afternoon and some, evening. I carefully calculated how I could take care of myself by not always being so busy. The end result, of course, was then when a busy time came around, I was ready, I was fresh and I was prepared.

I first put this plan into action by showing up at church on Sunday morning with an index card filled with spaces where I could invite teens and adults to meet with me throughout the week. Since I love setting goals, I set a goal that seventy percent of my card must be blank when I entered the church each week. Some weeks that was hard—but most weeks it just was the way I operated.

I wanted to meet with people, be in touch with them and be available to them. I always felt that this was the biblical model of discipleship. Still, I seriously doubt if Jesus had an index card! What we do know is that he was with his disciples, taking long walks, boat rides, eating together and just being with his friends. My passion for having this seventy percent idea continues to be fueled to this day. Having worked in the church for so many years, I had the opportunity of meeting with many pastors. I tired when I asked about meeting and they would go find their calendar and let me know that they could probably fit me in, *"How about three weeks from now? I think I can squeeze you in,"* to which I would also say, *"Hey, I will get back with you later."* Of all the careers in the world, I had always hoped that I would not be a pastor who would not have time for people. Of course, this is not just about pastors—it's epidemic in the world we live in today, and supposedly builds self-esteem for those with the busy schedules.

Joshua

Books always seem to appear in my life at the right time. At the same time as when I was adopting this lifestyle of being available, I read Father Grizone's book, *Joshua*. It is a fictional view of how Jesus lived his life going from town-to-town and house-to-house—he just had time to be with the people. I don't know if it was the occasional glass of wine that he drank as he spent time with people that got my attention, or the fact that people were important to him and that he had the time for them. Fiction or not, it became a part of my DNA because I wanted to spend my time being busy with people doing day-to-day life together.

I had to learn some new dialogue to make myself available and have a schedule more like Jesus'. When someone asked me if I could do something, I would often say that I was *"busy."* Little did they know that my *"busy"* was "busy doing nothing." I knew that most would not understand that my being out on my sailboat, taking a nap, working in the yard or just wasting time was all about taking care of myself. At first, I thought it seemed a bit selfish, and then I realized that the demands of my job in ministry at times could be 24 hours a day, 7 days a week, and I knew that I had to be mentally ready to be with people.

The Importance Of The Balloons

I had already made a decision that my career balloon was not going to steal time from my family balloon. I realized the importance of protecting my mind, being well rested and wanting to be with people, instead of believing it was a job.

The wisdom needed to create your balloons centers on your value of your own time. I think that it is important to stop and take time to enjoy the little things in life, invest your time in the right things and, most importantly, invest in yourself. The more you invest in your own mental stability and time management, the more fun you bring to the world. Allowing more time for relationships as well as time to slow down and ask God about your own life and how it's going from his point of view is a great start in the pursuit of a healthy life.

Time Management

In speaking with people about the progress in their lives over the years with implementing the Ten Balloons, the common response seems to be *"I do not have enough time to pursue my own hobbies (or some other balloon)."*

And so is the question the amount of time that we each have in the week, or the thinking and planning ahead that would allow a fuller life? Most people allow other people to direct their schedules and time. Sometimes out of necessity, but often just because it takes time to plan—and for a person who already feels stressed, there is no time to plan. It is a vicious cycle, or maybe a vicious attitude.

Don't We All Have One-Hundred-And-Seventy-Six Hours?

The first step in time management is taking time to reflect on your ten balloons. When you look at your current life, how content are you? Are you patting yourself on the back or kicking yourself? Wishing for something better maybe? Have you defined the overinflated balloon and the ones lying on the floor?

I offer a free and easy assignment for anyone who wants to make some changes. It is easy to do and you can do it from home—and if you are serious, a hundred percent success rate is guaranteed.

Change Your Life Assignment

You need a pencil, sheet of paper and about five minutes a day for one week. At the end of each day, record what you did hour-by-hour or even in half-hour blocks of time, if needed. Do this for seven days. That is, if you need that long, because most finish the assignment by the fourth day. Although you may have done this before—have you ever taken time to highlight each hour as related to each of the Ten Balloons?

Why do people stop by day four? Because they see the problem is not time but instead vision of how they use their time. The solution is not instant, but most people seeing a problem have a toolbox in their mind to solve some serious problems. People realize by doing this assignment that they do not need anyone to tell them what they need to do differently—they usually see it themselves.

Be careful about who you share your personal findings. Although you might have a spouse, colleague or friend that you might want to help you with this, you must remember that they might already be part of the problem instead of the solution. Sometimes I put on my *"coaching hat"* when I find people who really want to change, but just can't seem to be consistent in making some life changes. If you do get serious and need some accountability, be careful whom you select.

Setting your own life journey should really be a personal journey. I often hear that *"I have kids' schedules to consider, a job, ailing parents and so on."* I know that if I talk to them next year, or five years from now, that they might still have the reasons for not living the life they want to be living.

Combining Your Balloons

One of the greatest secrets of having a fulfilling life comes from learning how to combine our balloons. Let me tell the story of our purchasing our Lake House. Trust me, we never have had the type of income that you would associate with people buying a second home—but we did anyway because it fit into our Ten Balloon mindset. I would like you to see how simple life can be with just a little planning ahead.

The Fixer-Upper

- Buying a "fixer-upper" meant that in time we would realize a profit (Financial).
- We bought the house because of the arrival of our first grandson, and we wanted an excuse to be closer to him and his parents (Family).
- Once we purchased the home, we invited the children to renew some of their construction and painting skills that they learned growing up in our household (Hobby).

- The first few weeks involved Sherri and I throwing a mattress on the floor (Primary Relationship) as we made the house habitable.
- In time we bought a golf cart, which allowed for rides to the lake and lagoons nearby with the grandkids (Adventure).
- We bought a 21-foot sailboat, so our son Adam got to fish a lot. Sherri got to do a lot of meal planning and entertaining, which she loves to do (Hobby).
- The fireplace, the back porch swing, and multiple decks allowed for great times of reading and renewal (Mental).
- And, of course, the endless construction projects, swimming, and taking walks in the neighborhood (Physical).
- The uniqueness for us was that the house became "The School of Urban Studies National Training Center," and as part of my job, we invited small groups of individuals for two- or three-day trainings (Career).
- We were able to deepen relationship with many who were invited to stay with us at the Lake House (Friend).

One of the blessings that can come from hearing this story is that people realize that they are already doing better than they think. They understand that the process of *"combining the balloons"* is just a matter of thinking ahead and taking time to reflect and plan. We could have bought the fixer-upper with the intent of just making money, and although that is a great idea, for us, we knew that the house could provide more than a financial benefit.

Adventures With The Grandchildren

I would be remiss if I did not tell of how our adventures with the grandchildren have evolved into the ultimate in combining the Ten Balloons for our family.

Travel and adventure have always been a part of our marriage.

When the grandkids arrived and we took our first family vacation with our children and grandchildren, we knew that there had to be a better idea! A better idea than being with your children and grandchildren, you ask?

Because our grandchildren live an hour away from us in different directions, and we have had an almost unquenchable need to be with them, we knew we had a problem, or as some say, an opportunity. We discovered that when their parents were with us on vacation, they also expected to spend time with their children!

Realizing how important being with the grandkids is to us, I declared that we needed to take the grandkids alone on vacation. *"Since you have Tyler, Savannah, and Hayden the other three hundred plus days each year, we need to be with them all by ourselves for just a dew days."* Somehow, by the grace of God, they did agree. Over the years this has expanded into two vacations—and then three adventures each year—and thus Tyler, Savannah and Hayden have experienced much of the world with us.

Take Time

I often wonder how people can be so busy that they never seek a way out of being busy. I am convinced that in today's culture we must eliminate the *"badge of honor"* that we feel we have if we can tell the whole world how busy we are and spend time with your family.

CHAPTER SEVEN THE FINANCIAL BALLOON

I believe I was eleven years old when my mother introduced my sister and me to the Christmas Savings Club idea. I remember loving the concept because I received a coupon book, and each week as I deposited my twenty-five cents, I tore the coupon out of the book as evidence that I was paid up to date. Some weeks I would be behind, and some weeks ahead, based on my revenue flow! I loved my coupon book, knowing that in early December I would receive a check in the mail for $12.50. In 1959 that was pretty much like being a millionaire for a twelve year old.

Times have changed since then, and so have our expectations of our children. I doubt it was my idea to start the weekly trek to the bank. I am assuming it was a suggestion from Mom, but one of the things I knew for sure was that she nor Dad would be putting a quarter in my account to bail me out or to get me ahead. I don't recall if my friends had savings accounts. I only knew it was my responsibility to complete the task.

My life was filled with simple expectations from an early age. One of expectations was *"If you want extra things in life then you need to earn your own money."* To illustrate this principle, my dad called me into the kitchen one day during my freshman year to have a conversation with him and my mom. He reached into his pocket, pulled out a five-dollar bill and held it in the air.

"Michael, I want to present you with the last five dollars that we will giving you. From this point on, your mom and I will provide you with a house to live in, food on the table, and a few basic necessities of life. You will be on your own for the rest."

Translated, that meant if I wanted to date, wanted new clothes, wanted car insurance or even a car, they would all be my responsibilities, as well as the cost for any college aspirations that I might have. One might think that was a hard lesson to hear, but, ironically, I thought every kid in my neighborhood lived with the same expectations. I never thought it was a big deal, and looking back, I just thought it was a way of life. I often teach in my workshops with teens that if I could ever redo anything from my high school days, this would be it. I think this simple lesson has enabled me throughout my life to always believe that I could somehow *"figure out"* whatever I needed to with regard to providing for myself then, and for my family later. I was truly blessed by my parents' decision to not try to provide for my every need.

Making money came easy for me. I always seemed to have the "new best idea" for getting rich. My grandparents and aunt and uncle lived down the street from us, and I think they understood that Mike needed money! I could count on them for extra money just about anytime, and I think they could count on me for work that they did not want to do. It was really a perfect relationship. They always had grass to cut, weeds to pull, snow to shovel, and garages and basements that needed to be cleaned. If there was such a thing as minimum wage, I did not know about it, nor did they.

We never set a price beforehand—they just gave me whatever they believed the job was worth. Being from a different generation than today, they never had the idea of spoiling me and paying me for work that I did not do—or work done poorly. I wonder if they ever realized the importance of the impact they had in imparting the idea of an honest day's pay for an honest day's work.

My grandmother wasn't all business though. I remember many days of shoveling snow and then going into the house for some hot chocolate and cookies. In the summer it was homemade lemonade and cookies. I believe that she enjoyed baking them and having my company as much as I enjoyed eating those warm

cookies straight from the oven. In traditional grandma style, she wore her full-length kitchen apron all day long. When it was time for me to leave and get paid, she would reach into her apron pocket and pull out a vial of dimes. My grandpa did not smoke cigars, so I never knew where she got the glass tube that she filled with dimes. The tradition was simple. I would hold out my hand and she would gently tap out as many dimes as she deemed the work was worth. One thing that I never remember is wishing for more. The combination of cookies, the opportunity to work, and the coins in my pocket was more than any kid could ever expect! These work opportunities served as some of the greatest teaching moments of my life.

The Paper Route

For a few years I had a paper route. I thought all kids were supposed to have one, so I did. For six days a week, I always had something to do. I know my parents liked that because it filled my time after school since they both worked and only returned home in time for dinner. I didn't get rich from the paper route—but it was fun to always have money in my pocket. I only collected once a month from the customers, and I enjoyed this ritual especially at Christmas. I thought that making ten cents a week from each of the forty customers was pretty good. At Christmas, most gave me fifty cents, and some, even a dollar as a Christmas present, so you can only imagine how much I loved my job! I think that might have also been my motivation for the next year to keep and grow my paper route.

My newspaper customers also became my snow-shoveling customers. As today's students dream about snow days and school cancellations, so did I. My motivation was somewhat different though! Like a kid waiting for Santa Claus, I would not sleep well the night of a predicted snowstorm. I always wanted to be the first one out knocking on doors. My parents always warned me that I at least needed to wait until the sun came up. I remembering gently arguing with them in how unfair that was because some of my clients would decide to do it themselves, thus decreasing my income for the day.

If there was one thing I learned from my snow-shoveling days, it was that the harder you work, the more money you could make. By noon on most days I remember my body ached from head to toe but I continued to knock on doors. I wondered how I could do any more—and then I would reach into my pocket and feel that wad of money, and the pain would seem to go away. The older I got, my neighbors were willing to pay higher wages. I took my grandma's wisdom and never set a price with anyone. I just let them know that whatever they thought was fair, was fair with me. I am sure I could have asked for more—but job security was very important to me at an early age.

I know my life was not all about the money. I don't recall having great dreams for buying some big item or anything. I think I just loved the independence I had by being out of the house, having something to do and setting personal goals. My jobs centered on working hard and maybe, some would call it, *"becoming responsible,"* but since I didn't know that term, I guess I thought I was just having fun.

My parents left me alone somewhat in my moneymaking decisions. Back then, you could read in comic books about schemes that companies would offer kids to start their own businesses'. I think that companies that sold vegetable and flower seeds led the way. The company would send you an assortment of seed packages, and kids would go door to door to sell. The comic book ads made it look so easy, but there always seemed to be some catch to limit you from becoming a millionaire! I think by the time I returned all my unsold seed packages, I didn't even realize a profit. I do remember my dad asking, *"Are you sure you want to do that again this year?"* I guess that was to become part of my entrepreneurial training.

And yes, there were candy and magazine sales. I was in the Boy Scouts, and they always had Christmas and Easter candy sales to raise money for summer camp. I know for a fact that this was not a good idea. It seemed like I always ate my profits and had to suffer the consequences of not having enough money to pay the bill—oh yeah, that's why I had a paper route!

But times have changed. I often speak in schools to students, sometimes in the winter after a day off from school due to the weather. As we go through the workshop, I always figure out how to ask them what they did on their day off. I begin by asking how many went out and shoveled snow and made some cash. I might as well be talking to aliens, because it seems like it is no longer a value within families. Has something to do with the wind chill factor, safety, and needing the day off to sleep in!

When they get done laughing at my stories, they explain how the snow had melted by the time they got out of bed, or how it was a great day for video games. There is always the common issue of blame if they might hear my stories and think it is a good idea. *"Are you kidding me? My parents wouldn't let me do that." "Why would I do that? My dad uses the snow blower!" "I doubt anyone would let me shovel their driveway. I am only a kid."*

Growing up in Brooklyn, I knew we were not rich—and I knew we were not poor. Well, maybe a little poor. We lived in an apartment on Fifth Avenue near Eighty-Sixth Street on the second floor, with a toy store below. My backyard was the rooftop of the back of the store. Moving to New Jersey could probably be defined as one of my parents' greater goals in life in their pursuit of our having a yard and all the other advantages that they thought country living might offer.

Here Is The Last Five Dollars We Will Give You

I don't know if my dad intended to influence my life so much on the day that he handed me the last five dollars—but he did. And it wasn't about the financial peace, which I think was the point he wanted to make. The words that defined my future were *"If I have extra money, it is for your mom!"* Wow. He thought more about my mom than what car I would drive, or if I would drive, or about going to college. The unspoken message was loud and clear: figure out your own financial future yourself.

And it is probably the lesson I am most thankful for today. I see this giant void in our culture of children never having to figure anything out. It seems their parents have taken ownership of every aspect of their lives. From getting up to going to bed. What toys they have. Where they go (and if they have their helmets and shin guards on) to the cell phone checks that sometimes happen on the hour every hour. In the quest of growing up, parents today work so hard to deprive their children of being responsible for anything and so much has it roots in the financial aspect of our lives.

Twelve Dollars And Fifty Cents

Anticipating the Christmas check was almost as exciting as getting the check in the mail. My hometown back in the '50s and '60s lacked shopping malls and places to spend our Christmas money. Morristown was a short bus ride away, and my sister and I dedicated a whole day to being able to shop alone without our parents. My Christmas shopping list was pretty simple: my mom, dad, sister, and something for each set of grandparents, and that was it!

My memories of going from store to store and getting loaded down with packages are ones I will never forget. Of course, another great event of the day was lunch. At that time, Woolworth's, the original five-and-dime retail department store, led the way with the concept of eating at a lunch counter. I don't remember all that was on the menu, but I do recall the banana splits, milkshakes, and other great desserts that probably influenced today's fast-food culture. Eating at Woolworth's was always a special treat, but even more so without my parents. So I made sure to adequately budget for the bus ride, gifts, wrapping paper, and lunch!

It took me years and years to figure out the impact of this day on my life. I was never accused of being *"mature for my age"* as a kid, and maybe quite the contrary, as my undiagnosed ADD always seemed to lead me into some mischief or trouble. But for some reason, I understood at a young age that Christmas was not just about what I was getting, but also what I was giving.

My shopping trip was not my parent's idea. They didn't make a list, give suggestions, or use it as any teaching type experience. Somehow I loved the idea of being able to balance my budget so that everyone on my list got something—and, of course, I had lunch. Most recently, I have noticed that Christmas and other events throughout the year are almost void of children doing any saving and using their own money to buy others gifts. A sense of entitlement goes way beyond the Santa Claus years, where not much thought is given in how to say thank you and appreciate those in our lives.

Of course, this idea is no secret. I am not the first person on this planet to realize how self-centered our children and young people have become. But I may be one of the few to address it head-on with teenagers. As a youth leader in the '80s and '90s, we had a very large church youth group and a grand opportunity to impact lives.

Listening to the teens and their wish list became a frustration of mine early on, based pretty much on my personal experience. One year when I tried to address it in one of our weekly youth group talks, I realized talking about this at Christmastime was way too late. I always thought it would be good to help the students understand more of the idea of the birth of Jesus and what gifts could represent. But most of my message fell on deaf ears.

Thanksgiving Giving

The following year, I decided to focus on Thanksgiving with a three-week series dealing with the issue of thanks and what and who we were thankful for this year. At one of our meetings, we preprinted Thanksgiving cards and had each student take some time alone to write notes of thanks to their parents, teachers, coaches, and friends, which we would then put in the mail. It was quite a monumental task to mail over 2,000 notes—but we did it. I am sure there was some embarrassment on behalf of the teens when their teachers and coaches thanked them for the nice note—it was definitely a moment when our teens were becoming countercultural.

On another evening, we handed out paper and asked for them to write the names of the 10 top people they were thankful for—and the list could not just be family members. The teaching time centered on the idea of maybe making that their Christmas shopping list. I think it took them by surprise that someone would challenge them before Christmas to start planning for others. It was a switch in thinking about what Christmas could come to mean. I learned that not much could come out of one talk with teens—but presenting a series of common-sense ideas really worked.

We added a fundraising project and asked the students to fill up piggybanks for world hunger. I was overwhelmed at the response. It was their own nickels and dimes and some dollars that helped soften the idea that Christmas wasn't just about them. Since our group was large, we offered mission trips through the school year and summer. One of my challenges to the students was *"Maybe this Christmas you could ask Grandma for some cash instead of another pair of jeans that you probably don't need, and you could use that money for a mission trip."* The response was amazing—parents and grandparents loved the idea of investing in something more meaningful than traditional teenage gifts.

From the teens in our youth group, I learned a lot. I realized that is was not the selfishness of the teens that made their Christmases so self-centered—it was the lack of vision and support in making others a priority. I believe that far too many families have some of their esteem connected to presents given—and the idea if all the kids at school are getting this particular item, I sure would not want my child to be left out. I also smile when I think of that concept of myself growing up—for some reason my parents were not as concerned about what other people thought of their parenting ability.

The idea of Christmas again changed when Sherri and I got married. We had moved away from family and friends to begin our teaching careers in Chestertown, Maryland. It was one of the greatest decisions of our lives, and a time for us to *"figure out"* what it meant to be married. As Christmas approached, we decided to get a credit card from one of the only department stores in town as our income was barely enough for rent and needed items in setting up our household.

And you can imagine now the problem. We shopped for family and friends, and we knew our limits. But somehow with it being our first Christmas and wanting to make it special, we overspent far beyond our means. But as with all new credit card owners, the emotional impact of the shopping somehow blurs the possibility that a bill will be coming soon!

And so Christmas came along with all the wonderful gifts for one another. And then the bills came, and the reality that we had a long road ahead in paying off our obligations. We learned our lesson, and the following year—and ever since—Christmas is not our time of the year to go into debt. If you ask our children today, they would attest *"We never got anything for Christmas,"* but we know that is not true. Yes, we did buy them many gifts, (many inexpensive gifts so that they would have gifts to open). And they were also blessed because Sherri's mom must have been born just for Christmas day. We soon realized that it was okay for Grandma to provide the best gifts of Christmas, and we felt no pressure. I am glad that I was taught at such an early age to just *"figure it out."*

Getting Beyond Themselves

How do we confront this issue today? Is it really possible to have young people think beyond themselves in giving gifts to parents, grandparents and yes, even brothers and sisters?

I believe it is possible—but not by preaching or teaching. I see many young people doing acts of kindness during the holiday season and appreciating the impact that it has. But we all need to realize that doing good for others still needs to be translated into our lives on an ongoing basis, where we learn that being thankful is not just an event. I often wonder if some bank executive figured out the concept of the Christmas Saving Club, or was it designed to help people to be mindful of others each week and save on their behalf? Since there was no interest earned on the accounts back then, I am hoping it was for the good of others.

The Money Fairy

I didn't ask Sherri if she had a savings account when I met her. As a matter of fact, I met her when I was a junior in college, and one of the amazing things I quickly realized about her was that she had a checking account with money in it. I wouldn't say she had lots of money—but I think there must have been this *"money fairy,"* that would regularly deposit money into her account. Of course, I found that hard to imagine—always wondering when the *"money fairy"* would pass over my house.

She did things that I really did not understand. She went to the store and bought what clothes she wanted. She paid money to get her hair done and always seemed to be able to buy our dinner when money was a little short in my account.

So why would someone marry someone from what seemed like the wrong side of the tracks? Honestly, I never cared about how she got to that financial point in her life—and she was not concerned much about my finances—even the possibility of not being able to have all that she was accustomed to having. I gave her some baseless promises that she could continue some semblance of that standard of living. But then, when my first teacher's paycheck came along, most of that dream went down the tube instantly.

So why has our marriage worked for over 44 years? I sum it up that in spite of the fact that her parents Fred and Rose gave her money as she wanted, they instilled in her something more important: a work ethic. Sherri worked through high school and understood the responsibilities of having a job. Our common ground for marriage, then, was not so much the source of money—but the shared value of what money meant. When Sherri realized that she could not shop like before, it never mattered.

She quickly learned how to budget—just so that we could eat and pay the rent. It was hard starting out in marriage financially, but it was just a matter of changing priorities for both of us. Looking back, it is a time with some of our greatest memories.

What Do We Do Now?

But our finances were something we had to wrestle with as the children came along. What do we do? Do we give the children a checkbook—with a guarantee of giving them most of what they wanted? Or do we give them nothing and let them figure it out themselves? If it was a topic for debate, I think it would be tough for either side to win. We both liked how we were raised—yet we both appreciated the outcome of the other person's upbringing.

One of my earliest memories of helping our children with finances came when our daughter Andrea was about three years old and we were going to Kings Island, a local amusement park. For some reason, I knew that our budget could not withstand much more than the admission price. We knew of all the temptations Andrea would be facing once inside the park with the food, souvenirs and games to be played. I remember giving her some money in the park with the warning, *"This $3.00 is all that you are getting so you will have to make sure you buy what you want."*

Well, I might as well have been speaking in a foreign language because she had no concept of a dollar and what it could buy. She probably didn't understand that there was no more. But that was the day that we started having financial peace within our family. It ended up not being about Andrea that day, but instead us. I realized that Sherri and I were both on the same page, and although we probably each would have liked to buy her more that day, we did not. Looking back, I now see it was a day that we both compromised regarding our pasts without even knowing it.

When I say it started us on a road of not having money fights, it really did. In the years after that, we came up with a 50-50 plan. It seemed that Adam and Andrea always figured out how to make money, and we were willing to partner with them. As they entered high school I began thinking ahead. What if they pick the most expensive college in America? How could we honor that 50-50 promise? I believed if they could figure out half, we would figure out ours.

And so when people hear me tell my story, they think that I am suggesting that every kid should grow up with the five-dollar speech—but that is not true. I married the most amazing woman who had a different formula. How could I say which was right?

But I do think that having a plan is the important part. I recommend that parents talk about this with their children as soon as they are old enough to understand. Working with youth for all these years, I am still saddened to meet juniors and seniors in high school who still have no idea of what their parents are planning to contribute to their college education. Again, I don't think it matters if it is one hundred percent or none. What matters is that children grow up being better able to live up to the expectations presented to them.

Live Simply. Save Regularly. Give Generously.

I've always worked in jobs dominated by alpha males (military and law enforcement), but drive a 1999 lime green, two-door Pontiac Sunfire. I know this sounds strange to mention, but this often presents a problem when all of my peers are driving F-1 million pickup trucks—and there's the uncomfortable times when I get checked out by random dudes at stop lights. Yet it is the second car my wife ever owned, and we are both driving paid-off cars. Switching cars has enabled my wife Stefanie to drive our four-door car after our first child was born.

This simple approach to our financial balloon has spilled into other areas of our lives, including our house and even many day-to-day purchases. We chose for Stefanie to be at home with our children, despite her being a licensed registered nurse, and the implications have been huge. However, we have six months of expenses in our savings should a rainy day come, and we have money set aside so that one day we will be financially independent to pursue whatever endeavors we choose.

Most recently, I was offered a dream job, doing leadership development with small group leaders at the church I have attended since I was six years old. Pursuing this new career required a sizable reduction in pay—yet because of our simple lifestyle and our attitudes about what was important to us, we were able to take this job and adjust to a new lifestyle. The decisions that we made to live simply, save regularly and give generously have enabled us to now have a better schedule and the peace we cannot explain as I was able to enter my "sweet spot" for my career.

Matt, former Green Beret, Troy, Ohio

An interview

The Thirteen-Year-Old Entrepreneur

When did you start thinking about saving money? I think it began when I was about five or six. I got an idea that I wanted to save money.

Where did the idea to save money come from? I think the main reason I wanted to save money was to buy fishing things. We have a pond in our backyard and I love to fish. Now my idea of saving has changed because along with fishing things I am also saving for college and a car. I really didn't think about college and a car back when I was six because all I wanted to be was a cowboy.

What were some of the early things that influenced you along the way? Something that made me think about saving money is that from my house I can see about five banks. I realized that if I had a question about saving my money it wasn't a problem to go and ask them for some help.

So banks are important to you? I have realized that it is a good strategy for me to save my money in a bank—because I don't like bringing a lot of money with me when I go shopping. I am an impulsive buyer.

When did you learn about being an entrepreneur? I think I learned what an entrepreneur was when I was about eight. I learned there are many different types of entrepreneurs and in many different fields— and I say that because once I learned the word I realized that I already was one.

What is your business? What I do is sell salsa kits. It's not just regular salsa you get in the store—instead - you get to make it yourself. I just put all the ingredients in this package— tomatoes, peppers, cilantro, onions and my secret dressing.

ALSO, I don't buy any of the ingredients. I grow them all in my backyard—and they are all organic.

Where do you conduct your business? I sell them every Saturday in the summer at a local farmers' market in my hometown. I usually sell out—I think the people don't mind paying me a lot of money for my product because I am a kid!

Do you have other plans for your business? What I would like to do next is a bruschetta kit with the ultimate goal of getting it into large stores like Whole Foods and other organic stores.

I understand you have a lot of money in the bank? I have about ten thousand dollars.

Did it all come from Hayden's Homegrown Market? No. It's also came from birthdays, Christmas, other holidays, yard sales and my snow cone business at yard sales.

What are your plans for saving that money? I want to talk with a financial advisor and start getting into stocks.

What else would you like to do? I think something I would like to do when I get a little older is teach others how to save—and maybe be a motivational speaker and talk about it to other kids.

Hayden, Powell, Ohio, Young Entrepreneur of the Year Award - 2013

Chapter Eight

The Hobby Balloon

"Today is life—the only life you are sure of.
Make the most of today. Get interested in something.
Shake yourself awake. Develop a hobby.
Let the winds of enthusiasm sweep through you.
Live today with gusto."

Dale Carnegie

Dale Carnegie's words, *"Get interested in something,"* might be the best advice someone could ever give to the world. When I started teaching the hobby balloon to adult audiences, it seemed to be the easiest way to divide a group of people. Half of the room could talk for hours about their hobby, and it usually wasn't one hobby but instead many. It seems that there were not enough hours in the day for them to spend pursuing their passion — or possibly their latest passion. The rest of the audience includes those who have decided that hobbies were either for another day or another person. The overwhelming feeling is often that life is already busy enough and they did not have enough time in the week to pursue hobbies. The goal of this chapter is help readers discern what makes up their hobby balloon.

Sleeping as a Hobby!

When I explain to audiences that one of my wife's hobbies is to sleep I get an overwhelming mixed response. Many eagerly announce *"Amen"* and want an invitation to meet with her. Others think that sleeping is not a hobby but a necessity and are sure that it takes time away from a potential *"real hobby,"* or time to invest in the other balloons.

Sherri's story becomes an important lesson for anyone considering creating a balanced life. Sherri explained to me one day that she *"requires a lot of sleep."* For myself, I would say just the opposite. I seem to require a minimal amount. When I explained to her that I thought that was great and that we would just consider those extra few hours of sleep as her *"hobby,"* she laughed. She thought it was just sleeping longer, and I thought she was creating her hobby balloon.

Some have suggested, *"Imagine what she could do with those hours if she did not sleep. She could go watch television, go out and exercise, knit, cook,"* and the list goes on. The question, though, is not what others think she should do, but what does she enjoy doing? Sleeping longer makes Sherri feel better. Where I think we get lost in creating our hobby balloon is that we let others define what constitutes a hobby, or we engage in hobbies with possibly the wrong motives.

Not Understanding Golf

Many years ago, my good friend Deane invited me to join a church golf league. They played later afternoon once a week each spring and fall. I happened to own some golf clubs but never had used them before Deane's invitation. I saw this new adventure as a great opportunity to learn how to play golf and spend some time with colleagues in a different venue.

I didn't know much about golf when I began. Eighteen holes takes a long time. Golf requires talent. Green fees cost money. Golf is competitive. Scores are kept. And improvement is a goal to strive for.

And so one day, in the second season of hanging out with Deane, I decided it was time for a heart-to-heart talk with him. *"Deane, I really don't want to make you mad, but you know, I really don't like golf that much."* He was taken aback by my comment and took it personally, as if he could have made it a better experience. *"What is the problem?"*

"Well, Deane, it's not the problem, it's the problems. First and most importantly, I am a very competitive person and I like to win. Right now I stink at golf and do not want to invest any more time in it with the hopes of improving. More importantly, the money and time I am spending just to be bad at golf I would much rather spend with my wife and children."

I would consider Deane one of the greatest influences in my life as a friend and mentor. It was hard for me to tell him that I did not want to play with him. That decision became a pivotal point of my life in realizing what hobbies are supposed to be about. Deane understood, and we continued our friendship with our early morning breakfast outings, minus the pressure of my golf handicap.

At times I question the dictionary's version of a hobby: *An activity or interest pursued outside one's regular occupation and engaged in primarily for pleasure or relaxation.*

With that in mind, golf did not fulfill the definition of a hobby. I had another season in my life where I ran biweekly road races, and eventually a marathon. A marathon? Is that pleasure and relaxation? Another hobby I have is restoring old homes. Ever see the movie *The Money Pit*? Not sure I see all the pleasure and relaxation in that either. The key to the hobby balloon, as well as the other nine, is making sure that you define what you want your life to be made of. Although hobbies can be one of countless possibilities, it is crucial to define how large or small of a commitment you want to make in this area.

The more we understand the nature of the balloons, the easier a balanced life becomes. For the past ten years Sherri and I have taken just the grandkids on travel adventures two or three weeks a year. These probably could be described in our adventure balloon, but in reality, spending time with them fits the description of *"pleasure and relaxation."* Again, the key to successful living is how we weave our Ten Balloons together.

Guilt-Free Hobbies

I am always amazed to hear people apologize when they give up a hobby. *"I just had to stop running—my knees were so bad," "I decided to give up scrapbooking, it was just so expensive."* If we no longer derive pleasure or relaxation from our time investment in a *"hobby,"* isn't it ridiculous for us to feel we owe anyone an apology?

I can't even begin to count the hobbies that I have had, starting with my earliest memories with Cub Scouts/Boy Scouts and the seemingly countless hours invested in earning Merit Badges. I believe the genius of the Merit Badge idea was that it exposed scouts to new skills, new dreams, and to activities that might become our hobbies.

As an Industrial Arts teacher, I had the perfect career that matched my personality. My teaching tasks included: woodworking, mechanical and architectural drawing, metalwork, welding, plastics, electricity, wood carving, silk screening, home construction, photography, small engine repair, and arts and crafts. Just about every one of these, plus many others, are my become hobbies in one form or another.

A Life of Hobbies

Looking at my resume of 40 years, I see how so many of my early hobbies were natural fits for my careers. My background in construction led to building projects with the teens and adults within our youth ministry in Appalachia, New York, Chicago, Mexico, Jamaica, and Haiti.

A Ridiculous Amount of Photos

I had heard that some people grow their hobbies into something larger, but never imagined that for myself. I really looked forward to staying home to raise my children. With my first digital camera, and like most parents, I used to take ridiculous amounts of photos of my beautiful baby girl.

After taking countless photos around the house, I started taking a ridiculous amount of photos on our vacations. After my son was born, still taking a ridiculous amount of photos, I realized that I really enjoyed it and tried to take photos whenever possible, either of the children or things around us. I upgraded my camera and decided that I wanted to really understand it and know how to use more than just basic settings. A friend and I signed up for a photography workshop together.

I took the workshop and was amazed—and hooked. It opened my eyes to all of the possibilities that I had with my camera. I began to look for any information I could find. I joined my local camera club and started going on field trips. I started to really notice things around me and try and capture what I see when we travel. I've discovered that I love shooting landscapes and nature.

A close friend started a company and asked me to take some photos of their products for their website. The thought of people actually seeing my work made me nervous and excited. More and more opportunities started presenting themselves and I decided to try and make a small business out of it.

It's only been a year, but I couldn't have asked for a better start. I'm a featured artist on a canvas print site, a member of a creative team for a photography learning site, have sold multiple prints, and have had steady product photography work. I love animals and volunteer my time at our local animal shelter taking pictures of dogs to help them find homes. I'm excited to see what happens next!

Stacey the Photographer, Florida

The Air Conditioner Is Acting Up.
Oh No, It Is Micah!

In fourth grade I did not want to play in the band, but my parents had already decided it was nonnegotiable. I can't say I really enjoyed playing my hand-me-down trumpet that year—our private school band included only three musicians so it did not feel like much of a band! Begging to quit did not work. By high school I was hooked!

High school in my large public school included marching band for football, the pep band for basketball and a trip to Mardi Gras. Did I mention I was hooked? Then off I went to Vanderbilt with 150 new like-minded band enthusiasts. We opened up against Notre Dame and Lou Holtz on a Thursday night

ESPN game, and it was so awesome to play in front of a national audience and a packed stadium. The rest is history: Florida, Alabama, Georgia, Michigan and Louisiana.

I soon switched to playing the sousaphone. I would always practice outside the band hall, and my director later told me initially he thought the air conditioner was acting up when I started practicing! The Tennessee Titans moved to Nashville and played in our stadium for a year while their new stadium was being built, and I was invited to the opening game—with my love for football, I was living the dream!

My last college game brought sadness, knowing this stage of my life was over since I had decided not to pursue music as a career. I moved to the Washington DC area, got tickets to see the Titans and Redskins play in a Monday night football game and was amazed to see that the Redskins had a marching band.

My quest to join included many phone calls. I eventually got through to the right person, and they invited me to a rehearsal. I played with them and really enjoyed playing in a band again. When my schedule freed up enough a few years later, I came back to a rehearsal and kept coming back. Eventually the band granted me an audition and I was in.

I have been blessed with so many great memories from the bands, highlighted by the first time a boy asked for my autograph (which made me feel like a rock star), the first time I marched on the field in front of 90,000 fans, the time I caught one of the practice punts one handed with a sousaphone on my back while we were in pre-game formation on the field and the times I have talked to various players and coaches in the tunnel area and on the field.

I feel very fortunate to have had the opportunities I have had to explore two of my life's passions—music and football. A big thanks to Mom and Dad for the encouragement—they knew their son would someday become a rock star?

Micah the Musician

Chapter Nine The Primary Relationship Balloon

My Marriage Balloon Withered.

Something about the dancing equality of a bouquet of different colors on the end of a string—controlled by a child with a big smile—draws your attention and sets the world right. I believe that is why the image of the Ten Balloons was chosen to represent a balanced life. Throughout my life, I have found myself less than satisfied at times, less than happy and less than successful. In hindsight it is because my life was out of balance. One balloon was consuming more air than it needed, leaving others withered and lying on the sidewalk.

In one such time I spent a week in New York with a group of students and adults, searching for something to address my issues, and little did I know that it would come in the form of studying balloons! In this week of discovery and reflection I was able to objectively look at my life and notice the imbalance and shortfall. I realized it was my responsibility to fix it.

I returned home and began the hard work of backing out air from the over-inflated balloon and injecting life into the withered balloon so that it rose off of the sidewalk. The balloon that was over-inflated at the time was my career, and the balloon on the sidewalk was my marriage. I had traveled nine weeks the previous summer, taking kids to camps, speaking at different camps, leading leadership trips and adventures. I was only home during the weekends, during which I slept as much as I could, went to church (which was my job) and packed to leave again.

The effects of the summer began to play out in our marriage, and as clueless as I was, I couldn't see it. I returned home from New York with a greater understanding and determination to keep each of my balloons at a reasonable size so that I had enough air to spread around. The hard work paid off. Life is good. I regained balance in my marriage and have continued to work on it.

Seems like I now continually to adjust the air in my balloons. I'm not going to say that my life is perfect—it's certainly not. I like my bouquet, and like a child I skip down the street with a smile on my face, knowing that what I have is special.

Breck the Daredevil, Scottsdale, Arizona

The idea of a primary relationship balloon can take many forms, based on the needs, status and vision of each person. One of my great internal frustrations is that within our culture, families, churches, government and friends, it seems that everyone has an opinion of what other people's primary relationship should look like.

Working with young people, I have often seen years of frustration when someone believes that they need to be in a dating relationship. Their success in life is measured by whether or not he/she has a homecoming or prom date. With adults, family and friends have similar expectations, *"When are you getting married?" "I have this guy/girl you ought to meet."* And for those who have divorced, *"Will you remarry?"* Although most of the questions are asked with good intentions, they often backfire because people believe that they are missing something in life. Looking at the dictionary definition of a *primary relationship* is my suggestion as a good place to begin thinking about the primary relationship balloon.

> Primary relationships: are based on ties of affection and personal loyalty, involve many different aspects of people's lives and endure over long periods of time. They involve a great deal of interaction that focuses on people's feelings and welfare more than accomplishing specific tasks or goals (Wikipedia).

So, can your pet be your primary relationship? Can it be your brother and sister, parent or child, next-door neighbor or co-worker?

I think that the primary relationship balloon offers the greatest reason why we need to establish a vision for defining purpose statements for all of our Ten Balloons. If we don't, we allow the world to do that for us—sometimes with disastrous results.

Be the Best Ever!

Years ago, I heard a story from one of my favorite speakers, Tony Campolo, at a youth leaders' convention. He told the story of a postman and it went something like this:

> *"I know this postman who is probably the best postman ever. Everyday he ends his walking route about two hours late."*

Yes, he succeeded in getting the audience's attention—the best postman comes in late everyday?

> *"You see he has good reason for returning late each day. He stops to talk to everyone while he is delivering the mail, often checking in on the homeowners who live alone, many who have become his friends."*

And that story has impacted my thinking on so many levels—for myself and for those that I lead and teach.

- Any career can be the most important career. It just depends on how you live it out.

- Everyone needs to learn how to define success on his or her own.

You might be thinking that a story about career is a weird way to begin the addressing the Primary Relationship Balloon, but it isn't.

My Dad

I learned what I wanted from my primary relationship balloon from my dad. Growing up in the '60s, one of the popular paths to marriage was to go to college, graduate, marry soon afterward and then have some kids. When I explain that ancient-history idea to students today, we all understand how culture has evolved. But that was one of the popular paths to marriage back in the day!

I was a junior at Eastern Kentucky University, and our fraternity had offered to help the incoming freshmen settle into their dorms and tour the campus. Thanking God to this day, I was assigned to Sherri's dorm, and the rest was history. I would like to say that we had great intellectual conversations or we shared some common history or something—but truth is, she was just so cute and had such an amazing personality. Years later, she confessed that her attraction to me started with the fact that I was wearing my fraternity pin. Anyway, it was a match made in heaven. Two years later, I graduated, we got married and went on to teach, and soon after, Andrea and Adam were born.

Watching my dad was all I needed to become the husband I wanted to be. My dad had some great strengths—and some weaknesses. I made a conscious decision about which ones I wanted to reproduce, and which I didn't.

So, hearing Tony was that affirmation that I think we all need to hear. I wanted to be the "best husband ever." Just like that mailman, I wanted to define what success was and meet the mark. Everyday that mailman came back late—everyday I work to be the best.

Remember Paper Calendars?

I have had the opportunity to talk with hundreds of people one on one about the balloons, sometimes while I'm teaching, and sometimes just by listening. Talking with adults about their primary relationship balloon is not out of the ordinary. I think that most people have some adaptation of my *"be the best husband"* as their goal. Because, really, would you really write down, *"neglect my spouse"*?

Our conversations, for the most part, are short. Beginning back in the day when people would write down their daily, weekly, and monthly goals in some fashion, I would ask if we could look at their calendar together. Whether we looked at it or talked about it, my question was always the same. *"Where is your primary relationship on the calendar?"* It would not be an exaggeration if I mentioned that *"Ouch"* was the response for at least 80% of the people.

I Must Admit—I Only Attended Our Wedding

I must admit that I repeated the wedding vows. I must admit that at age twenty-one I had no concept of what for "richer or poorer, in sickness and health, and on and on," meant. I can only tell you that the goal for me was the honeymoon! Enough said. I soon found out that our primary relationship would look different when we were married than it did when we were dating. I found out later it would change again with children. It changed again with aging parents and now with retirement.

Define Your Own Future

One of the great things about getting older is that you do accumulate some wisdom, if you choose. When teaching workshops, I get most passionate about this topic of primary relationship because I think it is often the catalyst for the other areas in our lives. As early as the fifth grade, kids are under so much pressure to define a primary relationship. Whether it is a best friend or a boyfriend or girlfriend, it just seems everyone has an opinion.

Just Get Over It

Probably one of the greatest challenges that parents and adults present to preteens and teens is the idea of having a "best friend." Although the idea of the friend balloon addresses this issue some, it is hard to escape the external and internal pressure of fitting in…or not. Whether it be the classroom, the band room, or the bus ride home, helping young people understand primary relationship is crucial.

Parents' supposed wisdom is not always the best. Telling a teen to *"just get over it"* when they lose a boyfriend or girlfriend does not cut it at times. Since adults and parents have some of the same insecurities, it is hard for them to offer much help in this area. So what help is there? Unfortunately, parents sometimes attempt to step in and give advice like we might read in Ann Landers or some noted social problem solver.

What Would Happen If Fifth Grade Girls Ruled The World?

I wish that I could tell you that I researched the world and found the correct answers for what makes a great primary relationship, but I did not. Instead, years ago, I consulted with our fifth grade *Young Women of Distinction* leadership team and asked them to create principles that we should teach all of our Young Women chapters. I think you will see why I love working with this age group. Here are the seven that they wanted us to adopt.

- Keep your promises
- Don't tell secrets that I tell you
- Don't gossip and talk bad about me
- Do stuff together—just the two of us
- Don't put pressure on me to do bad and stupid stuff
- Treat me like you want me to treat you
- Like me the way I am

So what would happen if fifth grade girls ruled the world? They might suggest that the first "air" you can put in the balloon is working on yourself. Be a friend instead of worrying so much about who likes you and who is your friend.

Ironically, adults often need this bit of wisdom given to students also. I think that if primary relationships were easy, we would not have a divorce rate approaching fifty percent within our culture. I think that people would be happier and healthier if they would take care of themselves first before starting the process of trying to be in a relationship.

And just in case you have days when you think your pet might be your best choice for a primary relationship, read this:

SWF Seeking Myself

My parents were married for 56 years. My sister was married for 25 before we lost her to cancer. My three older brothers are in 20-plus year marriages. And me? I am single, never married.

You will not find me throwing a pity party. I am not bitter. And I am not lonely. I choose to be happy, and I find that I am happier than I have ever been! Sure, I would love to find my partner, but the truth of the matter is that I will not settle just to check the box "married." It took me years to fall in love … with myself. And because I am happy with myself, I do not need anyone to fill that void.

Is my life lacking because I am single? Absolutely not! I own my house. I have a rewarding career, and two extremely spoiled dogs. Most importantly, people who love and support me surround me, and they tell me that all the time. I have the freedom to pick up and go on a moment's notice. I don't hesitate to go to parties or events. I cook fabulous meals - no single-serve microwave dinners for this girl. I have babies that I love and spoil and hand back to their parents when they get fussy.

I have nothing against marriage, but being with or staying with someone who doesn't make you happy is no way to live life. I will carry on being a singleton and do so proudly. The single life is great. Just make sure one of your friends has a pick-up truck!

Katherine

My Friend Lena!

My friend Lena was an octogenarian and I was in my twenties when we first met. She was the matriarch of our very small country church, and all the members called her Aunt Lena. I was surprised to find out eventually that was a term of endearment and she wasn't everyone's aunt. Lena became my mentor and hero.

Lena's husband had died many years before I met her. She told of how he seldom went to church but would always get up and saddle the horse so she could attend church. She never remarried once he died because she had found *"the best one the first time."* I have been forever blessed by spending time with Lena—the way she lived her life and the lessons she modeled are invaluable. The church held chicken and noodle suppers each year and Lena led the way by mixing and rolling out the noodles. She used the excuse of cutting and serving the homemade pies at the dinner as a way to talk with everyone who attended.

Aunt Lena got up each morning and had devotions over a cup of tea. Her life was simple but so full of love and joy for everything. My goal in life has always been to grow up and become a Godly woman like Lena. Thanks Lena!

Sherri

Chapter Ten The Adventure Balloon

"The purpose of life is to live it,
to taste experience to the utmost,
to reach out eagerly and without fear
for newer and richer experience."
Eleanor Roosevelt

Growing up in Brooklyn meant that my world of adventure would begin on my tricycle. Zigzagging around on the black asphalt rooftop was where I spent many a spring and summer day. We entered the rooftop by climbing out the kitchen window, and the two-foot wall surrounding the rooftop was all my family needed to create our own version of a backyard. My parents attached a hose to the kitchen sink to fill up my three-ring inflatable pool. It was all I ever needed in my early years of play.

My view from my tricycle was exciting. I remember kids playing, noise from the traffic, and the big black tar bubbles that became my mission to pop. My world of adventure expanded and took on a new form when we moved to New Jersey when I was eleven. I could walk the shore of Lake Parsippany for hours and hours looking for fishing hooks, bobbers, and whatever treasures were there to be found. My greatest reason for getting in trouble with my parents at this age was losing track of time and wandering aimlessly around the lake.

During my senior year, the idea of adventure took on a new dimension. Family vacations and travel were really not a big part of my growing up experience. I am sure some of the reason was financial—but mainly it was because my parents were just content staying home. They worked very hard to own our home, and I think that they were just so happy to be there that they saw little need to leave.

I was in awe when a friend and I went to the New York World's Fair. I think the idea of not being with my parents, the exhibits from around the world and seeing things I never imagined planted seeds of adventure that continued to grow. Two years later, my friend and I headed to Canada to the World's Fair in Montreal. There probably have never been two people as unprepared to travel as we were. We had a car that might make it all the way, didn't have a roadmap and spent the first night in upstate New York sleeping in the car to save money we didn't have. Entering Montreal was like being aliens on another planet for two 18-year-old guys. The neighborhood we landed in did not have many English-speaking residents, and you can only imagine what three dollars would get you for a hotel room. I think I stayed up most of the night waiting for morning so we could pack our bags and leave.

The Roots Of Adventure

My turning point in adventure was my junior year in college. The work ethic my parents taught was beginning to bear fruit I never imagined. I came home each summer to work the painting business that my friend Wayne and I began as we entered college. I am sure we worked more than twelve hours a day and loved almost every minute. It was a season of great learning, adventure and maturing for me. Because I was paying my own way in life by this time, and college was part of the responsibility, I knew what I needed to save for school. Although responsible in many ways, I know I spent lots of money on dating and other hobbies that I probably did not need—I could have been saving more for the future—but I didn't.

Out of nowhere, I announced to my dad that I wanted to go to Europe before I went back to school. I wasn't sure of what his response would be, but I will never forget the look and the attitude he had when he said, *"I don't really care what you do."* He continued, *"It's your money."* He did, of course, give me a slight fatherly reminder that he was not investing in my college future, and I understood his point.

And so I went to Europe with what seemed to a plane full of grandparents. Since there was only one other person under the age of fifty, I was instantly adopted by everyone—and they all thought they were put on earth to protect me for the next two weeks. Because I was such an extreme introvert, many seemed worried that I would go off on my own adventures and not always stick with the group.

I see how my risk-taking makes me such an interesting case study in adventure. Having never ridden a motorcycle, I thought it only fitting to take my first ride through the Swiss Alps, all alone. I would wake up before the sunrise and walk alone through the canals of Venice and sit and stare at the statues in Rome. I slept in a castle overlooking the Austrian Alps and walked through some neighborhoods of Paris that opened my eyes to things I had never imagined!

I didn't realize it then, but my life was being redirected during that time. I read extensively on our bus rides and in my room at night, trying to read ahead about the adventures of the next day. I tried tasting every food imaginable, looked in every shop and business I could find and dreamed of not going home. In fourteen days I developed habits that have only grown on each adventure since.

I learned early in life that adventure does not always have to include an airplane, a distant destination, or a foreign language. Adventure, for me, became seeing how other people live, the things they do, the food they eat and the traditions that they follow. Today I call it my *"backdoor"* travels.

In college Sherri and I began our own quest of adventure in the foothills of eastern Kentucky. We didn't need a lot of money. I had a car, and we had weekends with not much to do, so we began just exploring anything and everything that was cheap. We married and moved to New Jersey and then to Maryland. We went to the Maryland and Jersey shores and New York City as often as possible. I built a small rowboat and we then had a new means of exploration on the Chesapeake Bay. Living on the income of a schoolteacher, we never imagined flying to places— but we could drive and drive, and drive we did.

Adventure became how we defined our family once we had children. We decided we were not campers after one rainy experience but learned how much adventure you can experience with little money. We never minded driving through the night for our Florida vacations and trips back east.

Adventure As A Gift To Others

Years later, we became the youth leaders in a local church. I soon realized that our sense of adventure was to be a gift that we could give to young people. Although we were usually on a *"mission trip"* with the focus on helping someone else, I knew that way more was happening than that. From Ohio we would head east or west, and I could never count the number of students who thanked us because they had never *"seen the ocean before,"* or, for some, had never even left the state of Ohio.

I soon realized that our youth ministry was more successful if it was away from the church and our community. I began to adopt the theme of "Seeing the world through the eyes of Jesus," and that we did. We would walk in neighborhoods where tourists never ventured, eat in coffee shops and greasy spoons, and meet the real people of the neighborhoods. Whether it was in the mountains of Kentucky or Tennessee, or in the cities of New York, Chicago or Dayton, we always could make an adventure out of nothing.

Over the years, I have taken hundreds of groups and thousands of students on adventures. My mindset became a *"backdoor tour"* combined with *"seeing people through the eyes of Jesus,"* and the rest became history. The quests became greater, not so much how far away we went, but in how we immersed our fellow travelers into the cultures.

- Can we go to the bottom of a coal mine?

- Could we sleep in a halfway house in New York?

- Could we sleep in an orphanage in Tijuana?

- Could we insulate five hundred attics in Dayton, Ohio?

- Could we build a preschool in Jamaica?

I find that we rarely go where the tourists go. We never eat at fast food chains like we do back home. We sleep on church floors, take cold showers and learn to do without—all based on how the people of the community live.

If you ask my daughter today about her life growing up, she will quickly tell you that although we take our grandchildren everywhere, we never took them anywhere! So we say, *"What about Europe, the Caribbean, Mexico, Canada and countless cities across America?"* Her reply is, *"Oh yeah, the only time we went somewhere was on a mission trip."* And to that, of course, we just laugh. The real issue, though, is that adventure is just part of our family—so much so that it might not have seemed like a special vacation. It was just one more day or week in our family.

Adventure Becomes A Family Value

And so what does a grandpa do when one day their first grandchild comes into the world? Tyler was born on a fall day in September. I must confess, infants are not my strong point—so while Sherri loved being a grandma to our first grandchild, I began having some serious conversations with God.

Each December, I invest a lot of my waking hours in thinking and reflecting on the past year, as well as dreaming and envisioning what the next year might include. This is when I take a serious look at my Ten Balloons and see if they need rethinking, then I set goals for the next year. Some might call it making New Year's resolutions. I don't—I call it living a balanced life.

Through my time, trying to figure out what it meant to be a grandpa that December, I recall feeling frustrated. I do not know that I had ever known any grandpas who had been an example I would like to emulate with my grandchildren. My own grandfathers were from a generation where kids were supposed to be seen and not heard—and I don't recall great interaction with them. I knew that they loved and cared for me, but it always seemed like it was from a distance.

As the time was drawing near to write down the goals for the upcoming year, I think God impressed on me that all I had to do was *"do what I did with my own children."* It sounded simple at the time, but grandchildren are not your children, and their parents have their own goals and dreams for them—and maybe the visions won't match. Tyler was about six when we decided he needed to go to Europe. I am sure many would say that was crazy, and *"how could someone that young get anything out of going to Europe?"* Well, I didn't argue with anyone. I knew the real answer—whether we took him to Ocean City, New York City, Europe or any place in between, we were not really taking him on a vacation. We were taking him to *"see the world through the eyes of Jesus."*

And then there were three grandchildren. We wanted them to meet people from all over the world. We knew how our children were blessed by being in the midst of diversity for so much of their lives. Our kids slept on floors, took cold showers, played with kids from many walks of life and it wasn't about being on a mission—it was about living life.

The grandkids started going on trips after their parents bought into the idea. We explained to the family as the trips began to grow that no one should expect much of an inheritance. We realize that if we would have saved what we have spent on five people traveling—well, you can do the math—it's ridiculous. And so the goal became not an inheritance, but a legacy with memories.

Combining The Vision Of The Balloons

Is it really just an adventure balloon? The beauty of living life with purposeful balloons is that you get to combine them. Imagine Sherri and I being together, (primary relationship), being with the grandkids (family), stretching our dollars (financial), studying about where to go and what to see (mental), and then seeing the world through the eyes of Jesus through our travels (adventure), and then you realize that life could not get any better.

As the grandchildren are getting older, we have always reminded them that they can opt out of going on the adventures at any time (because we are smart grandparents and understand that sometimes grandparents can be old, embarrassing and boring). It appears they have ignored that speech so far since they have opted to keep on going with us.

So each year, as I invest that December time by the fireplace, I attempt to discern just what might be the best ideas for the upcoming year. I learned, years ago, the idea of *"What is the best trip you have ever been on?"* My answer is simple - *"It hasn't happened yet,"* meaning that the trip next year will be better than the one I'm on now.

Who would have imagined as I sat on my tricycle in Brooklyn, watching the world, hearing the sounds and wanting to be part of the action on the street, that I would have been blessed to live a life of such adventure? And, most importantly, who could have envisioned the thousands I have been blessed to bring along on this journey?

An Interview

A Junior High Student's Adventure Balloon

Why do you think that adventure is one of your favorite things to do in life? Probably because when we learn things in school about people and places around the world, I can relate to them and I have a better understanding of what we are learning. It really makes learning different for me as I get excited thinking back of things we did and places that we saw—and even what we ate.

How much have you traveled? At last count I think it is thirty-seven states, more cities than I can count and eleven countries.

What makes traveling so much fun for you? One of my favorite things is traveling with my cousin Hayden. He is a year older than me, and it just seems we have fun every minute of the day talking and exploring. He really knows how to make people laugh! I also know that when we travel we don't always do the things that normal tourists do—and with my grandpa we end up always looking for the *"greasy spoon"* restaurants. They always seem to be out of the way from where normal people go. We also do a lot of walking and get to see how people live in different places around the world.

Does traveling always go as planned? No. We have a great history of what we call *"mishaps"*—the funny things we do along the way that we did not plan. One of them for me was when I was younger and we were driving in Colorado I got a little restless from all the driving and moving around so much in the back seat that I got tangled in the seat belt and thought I was going to die! They had to pull the car over and spend some time figuring how to get me untangled!

Another time my grandpa took Hayden *("Sparkie")* on a rafting adventure in New Jersey and it went bad! They had to walk through a swamp to get back to the hotel, and now every time Sparkie tells the story it gets bigger and bigger. But really, we saw the pictures that they took, and Sparkie did think that they were going to go *"out to sea"* to die!

What would be some of your favorite adventures? I have a few: Ocean City, New Jersey, New York City, Rome and Amsterdam. It is funny that each place is so different.

I love the Jersey Shore because it is like going home because we have gone there every year since I was one week old. New York City has museums and always a new restaurant to try. Amsterdam has the best French fries with vinegar, and we ate them while sitting on the street by the boats in the canals—and oh yeah, the endless canals. Rome has green parks, great buildings and cobblestone streets with lots of cats, and believe it or not, we traveled all that way and ate twice in an Asian restaurant!

Have you ever encountered any disasters while traveling? If you mean like hurricanes and blizzards, then yes! One time I went with my family to Turks and Caicos during a giant hurricane. We had to stay in the hotel for most of the day—but my dad went out and took some pictures anyway! But believe it or not I really wasn't that scared.

Another time we drove from Ohio to New York City. The roads were really pretty good all the way—until we got near the George Washington Bridge. There, we met up with the worst part of the blizzard. The snow was so high my grandma fell into a pile of snow when she was crossing the street! And believe it or not, a man was still playing his saxophone in Central Park while everyone else was sledding! We had a blast walking everywhere because even the taxi cabs were not running.

Do you have any funny stories from your adventures? When we went by Amtrak to Seattle my grandpa (Papa) had to sit by this really, really big lady on the train. Since we were in the coach seats that night, the seats were supposed to be our beds. She was so big though, that she took up both seats and Papa had to move around the train all night finding a place to sleep.

Traveling by train was really fun, and I like it better than planes. In trains I don't get claustrophobic because I can walk around. One time when we went to bed we didn't want to sleep on the top berth so we squished into the bottom bed and laughed until we fell asleep. We left the window shade up at night so we could watch everything going by. The lights outside were our nightlights.

Another time when we were in Rome and stayed in this really fancy hotel - we had to get two rooms because the rooms were so small. Papa decided that he should play a trick on us for some reason. After we left his room and got to our room the phone rang. We were really scared when the caller said they were calling from the front desk because they heard that there were children running in the hallway and they called to tell us to stop. The three of us looked at one another and were really scared I forget who figured it out—but someone realized that it was not a real phone call from the desk but instead Papa.

Of all the places you have been where would you like to go again? I would like to go to Rome again. We went to the Vatican and heard the Pope speak - but there was so much else to do in Rome we hardly had enough time to see it all.

Where do you think you would like to go when you think about new adventures? I want to go on a safari in Africa. From the pictures and movies I have seen, the people seem nice and the climate is warm. I really want to see all the animals in their natural habitat and of course I want to take Sparkie—because he is a genius and knows a lot about animals. I wouldn't even mind sleeping in a tent if it was new and clean.

Savannah, Seventh grade, Van Wert, Ohio

I Am Not Letting The World Pass Me By!

Don't you hate it when someone tells you that you can't do something? Or even worse, that little voice inside that says, *"no way can you finish that."* The seeds of self-doubt get planted and soon the world is passing you by.

I was that person. Then I found the courage to run my first marathon. I felt invincible when I crossed that finish line. The next day, I signed up for my next race. And that feeling of invincibility comes back every single time I cross a finish line. And I have crossed a bunch of them since.

I am not a fast runner. I am not especially athletic. I am particularly afraid of heights. But I love an adventure. Raft for seven days down the Grand Canyon? I'm in. Take a whirlwind tour of Costa Rica? Sign me up. Run two half-marathons in 6 days? No problem. If I want to do it, I will find a way to make it happen. I have banished those demons of self-doubt.

I love my job, but it can be challenging. So I need adventure in my life to keep me balanced. I need to get away. I need to explore or push myself physically in order to stay in the game mentally. And if I can't find anyone to go with me, I'll just head out on my own. No way am I letting the world pass me by!

Cathy

I Love Adventures That Impact My World View

Adventure is a necessary part of a full life. It breaks down paradigms, challenges beliefs, stretches physical limits, broadens worldview, and refreshes the soul. An adventure can be a variety of experiences. It is anything that stretches you, or is out of the ordinary routine of your life. There are big adventures: like a trip to another culture or country. And there are small adventures: like an afternoon of hiking, or going out to the ice cream truck.

Adventure keeps us young at heart. I am a woman who is very administrative, organized, and live by a ten-minute schedule. I prefer life structured and efficient. Those are good characteristics, but I also want to be a person who grows in flexibility, spontaneity, fun, and adaptability. So I open my heart to adventure. At times, it is scheduling time for rest and fun. I look for the little adventures I can do in one hour with little cost. It may be going to a park, trying a new coffee shop, just driving around with a friend, or taking the neighbor's kids down to the creek to look for frogs. If the seven-year old boy enjoys it, then it classifies for an adventure!

I also love big adventures that impact my worldview and stretch me as a person. These have room for more planning, and usually cost something. These adventures have ranged from a Saturday at the homeless shelter listening to life stories, to taking my teenage brother to the largest indoor water park, to living in Asia for two months to giving away thousands of books with Kids Read Now in my hometown! Seeing more of the world broadens our perspective and gives us a greater understanding of others and ourselves. And things outside our comfort zone, like cliff jumping (done it!), constantly stretch us as people. As I grow older and confront the demands of *"normal life,"* I realize more the need for adventure to keep my heart young.

Lorien the Queen of Adventure

Chapter Eleven The Education Balloon

I am not sure when I decided on the purpose statement for my education balloon—but from day one it has never changed. *"To learn whatever I have to learn to do whatever I want to do"* is probably one of the most important personal decisions that I have ever made it my life.

My professional resume includes a wide range of careers. Consider just some of my roles: coach, teacher, pastor, nonprofit director, consultant, motivational speaker and business owner. The common denominator has always been about coaching or teaching—but the venues have changed continually.

Consider this:

Worked in a Fortune 500 company

Contractor with the Air Force

Worked as a church consultant

Owned a house painting business

Started a T-shirt imprinting company

Worked as high school teacher

Trained college leaderships team

Coached 4-H and FFA audiences

Created three nonprofit organizations

"To learn whatever I have to learn to do whatever I want to do," allowed me to imagine succeeding in almost any career. When I combine my purpose statement with my risk-taking and entrepreneurial spirit, I understand my need to always be learning and changing.

At one time I worked as a youth leader in what was to become a mega-church. The church board made the decision to hire me knowing that I had an education degree, but not a seminary degree. As part of the terms of hire, I committed to enroll in seminary classes in needed areas. This idea worked for a season and helped me gain the confidence I needed as well as some credibility that the board thought I needed. I knew, though, that this was only the starting point.

I again realized the importance of my purpose statement when I went to Israel on a study tour. I was blessed to return two more times to the Jerusalem School of Biblical Studies and study alongside James Fleming, an amazing *"biblical scholar and archaeologist."* My eyes were opened to a new perspective of learning about the Scriptures like I had never imagined. It was an opportunity that included morning lectures in the classroom and follow-up afternoon treks across Israel with hands-on experiences from an archaeological perspective. Obviously, these experienced help me to gain confidence in making the Scriptures come alive to my audiences.

When I Grow Up

Working with young people, adults often challenge me with the idea that students are too young to know what they want to be when they grow up. And, of course, I agree with this opinion— sometimes. I do believe that many adults are living careers that were born in their childhood and teen years. Therefore, I want to help students design an education balloon that involves more than the schoolwork expected of them.

For me, the education balloon is one of the more interesting balloons to explore as it can continually challenge how we form the vision of the other balloons. For most children, teens and young adults the education path is somewhat laid out for them with clear expectations even as early as our preschool days. Adults, on the other hand, have to decide what their continuing education will look like after their formal education ends.

Linchpin

In reading Seth Godin's book, *Linchpin,* he poses interesting questions about our education system and its goals. *"The essential thing being measured in school is whether or not you are good at 'school.'"* He adds, *"Being good in school is a fine skill if you intend to do school forever."* But what if you are not a student forever? What if maybe you ended without a high school diploma? Or maybe received a college or advanced degree? What does your Education Balloon look like then?

In exploring this balloon it can be as much about what people are doing to advance their education, as it is their mindset about education.

I often meet people who announce with great pride that they have not *"read a book since high school"* or *"I don't read newspapers because they're full of bad news."* Which causes to me to wonder:

- Are you serious?

- Did your education really end with a diploma?

- Do you have children—are they embracing your values?

- If you and I were friends—what would we have in common?

- How do you learn about the world, the future, and the needs of others?

- Would you ever reconsider reading?

My high school experience learning how to read the newspaper with Mr. Perlett became not only the catalyst of my becoming more aware of the world, but also then led to the possibilities of how my future was to unfold through this additional education.

Straight A's. Honor Roll. Standardized Test Scores

Just how important are straight A's? How important is being on the honor roll or acing the ACT or PSAT tests? What about a vocational school or career center education? Aren't there many ways to define education? I believe it is crucial for individuals, parents and grandparents to wrestle with what they believe about education for themselves and for their families—and not to always rely on the current vision of our educational institutions.

Hungry for Education or Bored with Education

Have you ever heard about elementary school students who are bored in the classroom? Rumor has it that some teachers can't get the *"best out of my child,"* and, therefore, their education progress is hindered. More and more parents are taking the responsibility of education into their own hands for a wide variety of reasons.

I have mentioned already that I get to work with some of the best high school students in America. Or at least that is what their grade point average is supposed to be reflecting, but is it true? I meet with high school seniors who cause me to wonder how much time, energy and vision that they have with regard to education beyond high school. A few of the obstacles I have observed:

- Waiting until their senior year to begin visiting colleges

- Failing to research and apply for deserved scholarships

- Struggling to sell themselves to scholarship committees

- Selecting a college only to enroll as "undecided"

- Not knowing the GPA or test scores required for enrollment

- Unwilling to consider out-of-state education, although they might live closer to them than in-state schools

- Believing that because they were highly involved in high school sports, clubs and school organizations they have a greater chance of scholarships

- Missing out on the opportunity of Post Secondary Education Opportunities (PSEO)

Beginning Your Own Educational Mission Statement

Your decision to read this book may be part of your educational plan. Education includes *"a broad range of learning in which the knowledge, skills and habits of a group of people or individuals are transferred from one generation to the next through teaching, training or research."* I believe that one of the crucial elements involves our understanding in which areas of life we need education. As we look to the other balloons, we might realize we need education if we want to change our health, our family, or our financial future. Since education can come through personal coaches, workshops, online courses and countless other sources, we need to first dream the dream we want and then find the appropriate and necessary steps for gaining knowledge.

Education Defined

I was talking with one of our Muslim friends about her son, who was one of my interns as a high school student. In talking with her, I wanted to give her a *"heads-up"* that World Changers was a nonprofit and somewhat faith-based. I felt a need to reassure her that we are not affiliated with any particular denomination but that we did use the Bible for some of our leadership training vision. I mentioned that we do a lot more Old Testament teaching than New Testament, but we did both. Her instant reply was, *"That is fine. I am glad that you teach about Jesus. We believe that Jesus was a great teacher, and I think that it is important for my son to learn about different faiths."* It was great for me to hear this as I do enjoy studying Jesus as a teacher and leader. I tell all leadership students that you can study Jesus' teaching with a red-letter Bible that highlights the actual quotes of Jesus. I remind them that great leadership learning can come from studying Jesus if you pay attention to how He taught. He lacked a Bible, curriculum or workbooks—but he focused on storytelling and spending time with his followers. They traveled everywhere together, ate together and spent many long days and nights traveling from place to place. His model of education was not about getting a degree, but about the world as our classroom.

I Hate Computers!

I recall one day as a youth pastor, sitting in my office staring at this computer the church had purchased for me. Sally entered the room, quickly took off her coat, locked the door and told me that she was not leaving until she taught me how to do '"some of your own work"! Sally's boys were part of our youth ministry, which she loved, and she was determined that I would improve my image and "enter the world of technology." I didn't tell her about my purpose statement that "I would learn whatever I had to learn for whatever I wanted to do" because, honestly, I hated the idea of investing time in learning about computers because I thought I had "more important things to focus my life on than technology."

I really was not that old then, but it was all new for my generation and something I tried to avoid with a passion, especially since we were blessed with so many who were willing to help volunteer to make the church happen (like Sally).

My skills were terrible. My knowledge of the systems was zero. And worst of all, my attitude was terrible. She returned for many days, shut the door again and attempted to teach me a new skill.

In time I began liking the results. I learned to endure the pain of practicing the things I had been resistant to learn. I never took a formal class because I always felt I was so far behind already, and that there would be little hope for me in a class full of computer experts.

Time went on, and my skills and attitude did improve. I declared that I did not need a laptop. Never needed to get an iPad. Never needed to learn how to create a website. Never needed an iPhone. And, of course, you can now see technology was just one area of my life where a great amount of education would be valuable. Being an official *"senior citizen"* now, I know of some of my peers who refuse to use email, go online, have a smart phone or use social media. I realize how different their lives are from mine, and although I continue to struggle with technology, I am forever thankful for the day that Sally showed up!

Loving The World We Live In Today

It seems like that in today's culture we should be so much smarter than ever before. With blogs, TED talks, YouTube and the ability to Google anything or to ask Siri, education is so easy and so readily available to us. One of the greater changes in my world was the ability to download books because I just love to read. Little did I know that one day I would be writing a book for others to download on the technology I had tried to avoid.

To Learn Whatever I Have To Learn

When I decided years ago that this would be my purpose statement, I did realize the potential of how it would open doors in my future and help me impact the world in new and exciting ways. Over the past twenty years, most of my work has been through subcontracted projects, grants, short-term projects and jumpstarts.

One of those projects was an idea of Leib and Barb Lurie of One Call Now in Troy, Ohio. One Call Now is the leader in the telecommunications industry with their telephone notification system. I connected with Leib to take his vision of stopping the summer slide with third grade readers in the city of Troy, Ohio. His bigger vision was to create a program that could go nationwide. A vital part of the dream was to create a five-week reading and adventure summer day camp and distribute 10,000 free books.

Helping to bring *Kids Read Now* summer camp and the book giveaway program to life was one of the most enjoyable and satisfying projects I have ever worked on. The most interesting part for me was taking on the role because I was missing the knowledge base in some of the necessary areas. I was not a reading teacher, nor a reading specialist. My involvement with students had always been fifth grade and older, and not third graders, and, finally, it was a technology company, an area in which I can almost claim complete ignorance.

Kids Read Now

Our summer camp success was overwhelming. The reading scores of the 30 students enrolled soared by the end of the five weeks, and the book giveaway program grew from seven schools the first summer to over 50 in the next. And so how does that happen with a leader lacking in some of the basics needed?

"To learn what I have to learn to do what I want to do" is always part of my daily agenda. In the eighteen months that I was involved with Kids Read Now, I recruited volunteer teachers, reading specialists, project managers and people who came alongside me to dream this dream.

I was blessed to have so many educators from my past who, when I sent thank you notes of appreciation at the end of my tenure— forty-nine teens and adult volunteers helped make the program a success—from superintendents, to teachers, to parents and to students.

Through this learning process I learned how to take a local project nationwide—I created a team passionate to help pioneer the idea of getting thousands and thousands of books to students through the mail, and a plan of accountability to help increase reading enthusiasm as well as reading scores.

Showpig.com

Soon after working with Kids Read Now, I took a new challenge in working with *showpig.com*, an online auction company for pigs. Showpig.com is what I refer to as eBay for children, teens and families that show pigs at county and state fairs across America. My initial job description included staff development and taking the owner's ideas and helping to create the needed systems for a business that today runs over 900 online auctions. Again, I lacked what some might say were the key qualifications for the job. I knew nothing about pigs, or the show pig industry, and I knew nothing about online auctions. So again, how does that work? The learning curve was gigantic, as the role of the position became to double the size of the staff and double the number of auctions in eighteen months. It seemed like I was reading a book a week to catch up on some needed business skills and trends within our culture. Sherri found it amazing when a farm magazine arrived in our mailbox. Sometimes I wonder how a kid who grew up in Brooklyn would now be trying to figure out livestock issues in the Midwest. My role within the company included coaching the staff to ensure that we were providing excellent customer service as well as coaching for our staff in both their professional and personal levels.

I believe that my confidence in succeeding came from the fact that I have always know that I have so much to learn about so many things. Knowing that my life has been a succession of successful roles based on the idea that I had *"to figure stuff out,"* it seems like nothing is impossible.

What is exciting to me about education is that it never ends— unless you decide you already know enough.

Life In A Mill Town

Education has always been very important to me, and I worked hard to excel in school and received a scholarship to Furman University. During college, I began to think more about what I was going to do upon graduation. I decided to use my leadership skills and love for children during college, and stepped out in faith to make a difference within the Greenville, South Carolina community.

Through high school I had been involved in an afterschool children's program called Clubhouse. I decided to start my own Clubhouse as a sophomore in college. I fell in love with it. I fell in love with the children and their families. It became obvious by the time I graduated that this is what I was meant to do. Upon graduating, I raised funds, put together a board of directors, and created my own job as the director. We opened two more locations in other neighborhoods in the next two years.

Clubhouse was and is a calling—not a steppingstone—for me. Working with Clubhouse led me to want to live in the neighborhoods where the Clubhouse kids lived. Upon graduation, I rented a small mill house in the neighborhood. These experiences led my husband and me into becoming foster and adoptive parents.

Clubhouse led me to partner with local churches in Greenville that hosted the ministry. I started to fall in love with the local church in a new way and realized the next step in my journey would be to serve as a pastor and preacher. I became the part-time licensed pastor of a small congregation of about 15 people. I requested to be appointed to a historically black congregation because of my relationships with the children of Clubhouse.

I became convinced that if I was really going to do this pastor thing well, then I needed to go back to school and get my Master of Divinity degree to pursue ordination. I had been taught if I was going to do something—aim high.

When I graduated in 2007, I was sent to my second church appointment, also in Greenville. I believe that my career will always be evolving, and I am open and can envision a number of different shapes that my career/calling could take in the future. No matter what form my calling takes, my purpose remains the same—to serve God's people, especially children, youth, the underserved. I am thankful that my family believes in me and supports my quest to respond to this calling. I often sum up my passion by the words of Frederick Buechner, *"The place God calls you to is where your deep gladness and the world's deep hunger meet."*

Pastor Christie, Greenville, South Carolina

Learning On The Farm

Six months or so into our marriage my husband and I purchased a tent. We set it up in the yard and sat in it, dreaming what the rest of our lives would look like. A couple years later we started on the having kids part of the life we dreamed up. About six months into that idea we realized we didn't know what we were doing and figured by the size of my belly we better come up with a plan. So we hatched this idea, we would volunteer to teach the kids in our church, find the ones we liked best and do what their parents did. The first thing we realized about these kids was that we did not know their parents, because they were busy spending time with their kids, not us.

Purposefully engaging in relationship would be the most important ingredient in our parenting plan. What happened next was a natural process that would be interrupted by my preconceived ideas about how education should look. I instinctively began to teach. My first little baby by three months old experienced me in her face with colored cups cooing the names of the colors over and over. Eventually the time came to start thinking about her *"formal"* education. Those parents we had found years before did this really crazy thing we had never heard of and weren't even sure was legal. They homeschooled their kids!

In time I gained confidence that I could engage my daughter in a learning process that would be uniquely tailored to match her interests. My children's education would not be a distinct facet of life that they dreaded. Rather learning would be a lifestyle that would unfold within the framework of our relationships. Education would be part of daily life rather than an interruption. Some days were hours with math books, some days were reading books in our makeshift covered wagon, one year was spent building our house ourselves while sleeping in a tent by the creek. As the years have unfolded, we have never yet found that age we don't really like. As the kids grow older and their interests change, they now possess the tools to learn what they need to accomplish their new goals. Life has taken many twists we could not have dreamed, and spending our days together has been an even better life than we could ever have dreamed up.

Beth Ann, Educator, Kentucky

Growing Up In Jamaica

Growing up as a boy in the community of Hopewell, Jamaica, was at times a stimulating experience. The many challenges that a young man like myself had to deal with throughout the life cycle were overwhelming at times because I had to deal with physical, emotional and psychological changes as I grew up. There was no existing manual for growing up, except for the rules and regulations laid down by my parents and educators in the formal educational system.

Very few options were given to me as a child, due to the fact that my family was not well off, and many times I often felt confused and lost. My parents did the best they could to provide guidance and were there to help navigate me in this confusing world. They did not shirk in their duties in spite of their financial and economic setbacks.

In 1981, my encounter with Rev. Delbert Blair changed my life for good. Rev. Blair became a mentor and a father figure in my life. Many times he sounded stricter than my biological father, but looking back now, I see the good that he has done. He is an individual who tosses you into stuff and says, *"Go learn,"* and because of this, today I can do so much stuff that at times I even amaze myself. He helped set me on a path of how to live a life of faith—and then put it into action to benefit others.

My educational journey has been extensive and a priority of my life. I started my educational journey at the Bethel All Age School, The Kenilworth HEART Academy, The College of Hospitality and Vocational Skills, Caribbean School of Business, Royal Caribbean Institute and am currently pursuing an associate degree in social work at the University of the West Indies Campus in Montego Bay, Jamaica, and a diploma in psychology/social work at the Stratford Career Institute in Canada as well as a diploma in gourmet cooking at the International Career School of Canada.

In August 2010 I was honored and privileged to be selected to participate in the United States State Department's prestigious International Visitor Leadership Program, to examine the role of government, cooperation and NGOs in supporting civic engagement as well as the use of media in promoting and facilitating citizens participation in the United States of America. I got the chance to visit the White House and other legislative buildings in the US Capital, as well as visiting over nine other US cities. I will never forget this experience as it helped me in my pursuit of continual education.

I have a passion for community development - hence I have many years of experience serving on many civic, religious and community-based/nonprofit organizations. I consider myself as a youth-oriented individual who emphasizes the balance life concepts, spiritual, social, mental and physical and has put service to humanity above self and is a very concerned about the welfare of the member of community and the wider society.

I am committed in seeing voluntarism becoming an integral part of the consciousness of Jamaicans and am equipping myself to continue working with professional organizations where we are able to utilize our abilities to pursue social change that will improve the quality of life and development of the potential of each individual, group and community within our society.

Oral, Hopewell, Jamaica

Chapter Twelve The Friend Balloon

The topic of friends is the one most difficult to address in a world where so many people already have hundreds and hundreds of Facebook friends! Hmmm. Well, maybe we need to figure out our own vision in this area. I thought it might be good to start out by exploring a few key questions that I ask of teens on the topic.

- Can you really have more than one BFF (Best Friend Forever)?

- Have you thought more about being a friend than having a friend?

- Do you realize that friendships can change with the seasons of our life?

- Do you know what you need from a friend?

- Do you often sing "Friends are friends forever"?

- Who can you call (outside of your family) at 3:00 a.m. when you have a need?

- Have you invested enough time falling in love with yourself?

The idea of friends and friendship will have an impact on the other balloons, based on your age, season of life and attitudes about yourself and others. Establishing what you really believe about friends will have a great impact on your other balloons.

Best Friends?

I do take issue with our education system about one word in the

English language. With eight years of English studies prior to high school, you would think that someone could teach students the definition of the word *best.* Look, for a moment, at the definition: *Greatest, finest, foremost, leading, prime, first, chief, principal, highest, top, second to none, matchless, unbeaten, and perfect.* If you apply any or all of those words to someone you might be calling a best friend at the moment, how is that looking?

The popular phrase BFF became prominent in written works from the 1980s onward and continues to this day for students as well as adults. In conversations with students they are eager to tell of how many BFFs they have, only for anyone to ask them the question, "How can that be—do you understand what the word best means? Don't you mean you have one best friend?"

Why should we worry about what seems like a junior high issue? Because if I am in junior high and I lose my best friend, I might think the end of the world is approaching. For a teen it is no different to them than what losing a job or getting a divorce might be for an adult. Parents and adults downplay this issue too often. I believe that parents and those in connection with young people need to help young people through this issue. Unfortunately, some adults have not yet figured out this relationship in their own lives.

What happens to the teen after the balloon pops? The similar question arises as with any balloon popping. What will I do now? What will others think? What did I do wrong? What will I do now that I am alone? One of the solutions comes from answering the question: What about the other eight or nine balloons? Is there more to life at the moment that I can focus on?

Wayne

I happened to a have a best friend in high school. I realize that might sound weird to point out that I had a best friend, but the reality is that in life we do not always have a best friend every day and in every season of our lives. The potential for seasons of change is always there. Wayne and I ran track, cross-country, and wrestled together for a big portion of our high school careers. For a season our girlfriends were very close friends. We worked a summer job, building swimming pools and started our own painting business together. My life was blessed a million fold because of our relationship. We held each other accountable to a higher standard of high school living without even mentioning it. I am pretty sure we never once had a conversation about *"being friends"* or *"being best friends"*—it just happened.

Wayne went to college in Illinois while I went to school in Kentucky. We remained in regular contact during our freshman year—but slowly we grew apart because of distance, difference in college and career goals and eventually, marriage. I have never looked back once in regret about the change in our relationship because of who I became through our relationship. Most of my success today came through the seeds planted in high school. Without really understanding the concept of the Ten Balloons then, I now realize that together we were doing an amazing job in building a foundation for life. We developed a strong work ethic, independence, respect for our girlfriends and our parents, a sense of adventure and financial responsibility—and living life to its fullest.

College

And so in college, being in a fraternity offered an opportunity to have many close friends, sometimes called associates, because of the common bond that a fraternity offers, but nothing to the extent that Wayne and I had. I also realized that I did need to replace that relationship with a new "best friend." My high school years helped develop a confidence in me that was not dependent on whether or not I had a BFF.

I Didn't Marry My Best Friend

Now, I have heard that some people *"marry their best friends,"* and I totally understand the concept, but that is not the case with Sherri and me. We met during my junior year in college, and I guess I never had the concept of her being *"my best friend"*—I just thought she was my *"lover!"* Of course, if I would have learned the definition of *best* from my teachers, then yes, all of those words describe her, and I should have been calling her my best friend. And so forty-four years later when I hear that people are still married to their best friend, I just think to myself, oh yeah, and I am still married to my lover! I also saw in college even less of a need for another best friend because of all the time and energy Sherri and I invested in one another.

Working with teens over the years, I decided it was important for me, at times, to proclaim that I currently do not have a best friend. "And as a matter of fact, I have not had one since Wayne." I study the reactions on their faces, and for some it is like I just gave them a million dollars. So many people live so much of their lives in a quest for a best friend that they ignore all the great relationships that they might already have around them. I believe that life for many would be so much easier, young people and adults, if we could just relieve the pressure they feel about their Friend Balloon.

Being A Friend

One of the hardest lessons that we have to teach our children and grandchildren is that they cannot expect to automatically have a friend or a best friend. Friendship is not a rite of passage - it must be earned. It is crucial that we all learn how to be that friend or best friend. One of the challenges in our culture is that parents are not always able to teach this principle because they struggle with this need for friends themselves. It is often discouraging when I hear a parent say that their child is their friend or best friend. I believe that children need their parents to be parents instead of friends. I know for me it was always my goal to be lifelong friends with my children—but that process would begin when they were 18 and left the house, and our relationship changed. I believe parents offer children a completely different agenda and expectations than friends.

In my four decades of working with youth I have never seen the personal devastation of many young people because of the concept of friends like this generation. We have been raising children to be so self-focused, with the example of our teens taking *"selfies"* at least once a day to show the world how amazing they are. I believe that our social media hinders the idea of real friendships and building best friends. There is a great need for people to get as many *"likes"* as possible, based on their most recent posts.

Look Into My Eyes When I Am Talking To You

Probably the most painful workshop that I teach is my communication workshop. The goal is to teach participants to have meaningful conversation with one another, and the challenge is equal for youth and adult audiences.

I have been blessed to work with some of the most amazing academic students in America, only to find out that as a high school junior or senior they cannot have a two-minute, meaningful conversation in which they actually show care for the person they are talking to. They have been empowered to wait for people to talk to them—ask them questions—and have no vision that the conversation is two-way. Most students are willing and able to tell about all their advanced classes, special teams, awards won and maybe their favorite movies and music, but beyond that, their ability to have a conversation is minimal. Wondering how that happened? Think about the last ten conversations that you have had with an adult—how many questions did they ask you? I believe that for most people, the art of conversation is a lost art, or one never experienced by many.

The amazing part about the communication workshop is that within two or three hours we can begin to change the attitude and skill level of our teen and adult students. Ten years ago I created this workshop for fifth grade students, and the results are amazing. I found that the younger we begin teaching this, the fewer bad habits need to be changed, and the energy to fuel the conversations increases within the room. One of the most crucial starting points is to have participants look into one another's eyes as they are talking. This idea, of course, receives lots of moans and groans and resistance when presented, and also a sense of disbelief.

> Have any of you ever been in trouble at home? Have your parents ever had issues with you and started lecturing you? And you respond by looking at the floor while they are talking. And they say, "Look at me when I am talking to you." And you, if smart, do not say, "Why? I listen with my ears, not my eyes, and yes, I can hear you." Has this ever happened to any of you?

Of course, the answer is yes. It doesn't have to be with a parent, it can be a disagreement with a friend or associate. But our natural reaction is to look away.

Many, of course, are surprised this is a universal situation. They believed that it only happens them. I then get their attention in a new way on the path to helping them succeed. *"Well, you know, you who believe that God created you, then you can blame Him (or Her to some audiences)."* The response is universal. Our brains believe that if we can disconnect from you by not looking at one another, then the bond is broken. The eyes serve as this link with our bodies. When we look at someone for the first time with affection, our entire body responds when we look into one another's eyes.

It is a fun topic to deal with, but also one that is crucial. I ask them if they have ever had a teacher, a parent or adult in their life that looks at the ceiling or off in the distance when they talk to them. It seems that they can all name someone. And the question is, if you remember them, what do think about your ability to connect—or not—through your eyes?

Unfortunately, we have lost the dinner table in America, where we have opportunities to have regular conversations as a family. Conversations as we eat in fast-food restaurants or eat drive-thru meals in the car just don't cut it when compared to meaningful, face-to-face conversations. We live in a culture that offers lots of car and van travel time that could be translated into the most amazing conversations, but instead we have headsets on: video games, television and the potential of no meaningful conversations. I think in our busy world we need to rethink how to teach and practice communication skills with our families. When I suggest that when families go out to eat that everyone leave their cell phones and video games in the car, I get the response that I must be an alien or something!

Who Would You Call At 3:00 A.M.?

I had the opportunity to be on Lyman Coleman's workshop team years ago. At that time he was a leader within the church world in how to effectively create and lead small groups. He would go to churches and in the several day workshop would have the participants live out the formation of a small group. I was invited to go to Michigan and pioneer it with him with leaders of youth ministry because that was what I was doing within our youth ministry at that time. It was one of my shorter careers. I loved every minute of the trainings—but our children were young and I did not want to be on the road that much at that time. Being blessed by what I learned from him, I have continued to follow his example—and the reason I tell his story is because I believe it helps determine what it means to be a friend.

"Who would you call at 3:00 a.m. (other than family) if you had a need—even if they lived five hundred miles away?" His simple

statement became somewhat of an acid test for me to see that meaningful relationships, friends and even best friends do.

Whether you define your Friend Balloon with a best friend, lots of friends or lots of associates, it is your balloon to define. The goal will nearly always be internal instead of external. Instead of wondering why people are not reaching out to us as friend, we often need to ask ourselves what we are doing. Some people will open a conversation with me by saying, *"I haven't heard from you in a long time and I was wondering what is up."* Depending on the relationship, I sometimes ask them (but more often just think it), does your phone only receive calls? I have learned not to own other people's issues about relationships.

Seasonal Friends

When I think of seasonal friends, I remember our first year of marriage when we moved to Chestertown, Maryland, to be teachers. We soon connected with fellow teachers and discovered fun things to do as couples as we all were without children. For us it was a new type of friendship. As a group, we had a lot of give and take, lots of personalities and expectations involved, but at the end of the day we knew we had developed a level of friendship in which we could share some common experiences. I do not think that within the group anyone had a need to be best friends, and for me this turned into a new understanding of the Friend Balloon.

Our life changed with children. We probably didn't have as much time to build relationships as before, but now we became friends with the neighbors. Our roles changed as friends. We were looking out for one another's children, sharing snack time and an occasional mealtime with other people's children. Our "adult time" was usually standing in the driveway, talking about life and raising children. It was a new shape for our Friend Balloon. If we needed help with something or had an emergency, we knew we could count on someone in the middle of the night.

I believe that a starting point for people as they get serious about defining their personal balloons is to identify your current season in life. We didn't need to stay in contact with our college friends, our teacher friends, or our neighbors. We hold dearly to all of those memories and are so thankful in how all of those people helped us mature as people. We are thankful how such a community of friends blessed our children.

Some people will live in the same community for their entire lives, and their Friend Balloons will look different. Again, it is always crucial to define your own balloons based your life season— whether you are changing careers, getting married or divorced, moving to a new neighborhood, or pursuing new hobbies. The goal must always be assessed by how I am as a friend—as compared to measuring whom my friend is today. If we can teach our young people the value of being a friend, I believe that their lives will always be blessed with good friend relationships.

Do your Friends Define You?

What happens when we realized that friends are just a part of our identity? This is true of all the balloons. Even if we can't walk down the street holding hands with a best friend, go to the bar or ballgame with a best friend, or even have someone to tell our deepest secrets, it's okay.

Our balloons are not all the same size for a reason. Some people have a greater need for social interaction. Some need people to talk to—others to have someone listen to them. We are all unique.

Healthy Relationships?

What really makes up good relationships? What are good boundaries? When are we in an abusive relationship and need to get out? Countless books and resources are available in these areas that some might need to consider.

I always believe that there are times when we do need help in defining our own balloons. We need to seek wisdom when we realize that maybe our relationships are not helping us. Although we are the ultimate decision maker about our own lives, often in times of crisis or need it becomes crucial to reach out to those who might offer a new or different perspective.

Dumpster Diving Friends

Our beachfront hotel room was filled with the hum of the blow dryer in the background and the smell of the ocean coming in the cracked window when the phone rang. I continued to get ready after another relaxing day at the ocean. A day spent reminiscing and laughing with my best friend. We were there to celebrate our fortieth birthday and over thirty years of friendship.

She hung up the phone in a panic after learning that she needed a paper ticket to fly home, but it had been thrown in the trash by the hotel staff. My ticket was electronic and hers was not! Our plan was to borrow flashlights and head to the hotel dumpster in the dark!

When we found her ticket in the very last bag in the dumpster, we celebrated our victory with cheers! You would have thought we had found a million dollars. We realized one more time that we would do anything for each other—even dumpster diving.

Now, let's rewind thirty-one years. Heather and I met when we were in the fourth grade. We were inseparable from day one. We could not be more different, but somehow we found a way to respect our differences and accept each other for who we really were. We spent every weekend together, sleeping over at each other's houses, driving our siblings crazy, and dressing alike. We survived boys and mean girls, and traveled together on vacations and mission adventures across the country and around the world. Heather moved to a new school in seventh grade, but it did not slow us down. In fact, it brought us closer. I think our shared values and faith allowed us to be happy for each other and offer one another perspective. I don't ever remember jealousy between us, rather a true feeling of wanting each other to succeed. We had the best high school experiences together. We had planned to room together in college, but God had a different plan. We went on different paths, and soon both married and began our own families.

We have built a bond like sisters over the years. We have lived in each other's best stories and memories. We make time to talk, spend the day together, and have lunch. During different seasons of life, we might talk five times a day or every other week. We know we can always just pick up where we left off though. I am so thankful for my dumpster diving friend!

Carey, Springboro, Ohio

The Disrupter Of The Status Quo

No one would ever accuse me of being a big dreamer. I tend to hold my cards close to my vest, continuing to process information until I am satisfied that I can achieve a desired result. I am the kind of guy who is never confident unless I am holding a royal flush—a risk avoider if ever there was one. I once read that *"If you don't have a big dream, attach yourself to someone who has a big dream."*

I had heard about a youth leader at a growing

church long before I actually met him. However, I was able to observe the results of his work with three high school teens in the town where I lived. These teens had something special about them, as they were not self-focused like many of their peers. They were about making a real difference in their school and in their community.

Years later, I met this guy at a workshop in Columbus, Ohio, and everything he and the two young ladies leading the sessions said fell in line with my belief that teens are the most underutilized resource in our nation today. I, like he, believed that given training, encouragement, and opportunities, teens could accomplish amazing things.

Our friendship over the years has deepened through countless hours spent together, dreaming, acting out the dreams, and developing a high level of trust with one another. My dreams have grown bigger. I know that I am on to something when I share one of my ideas and he asks, "Whom have you been hanging out with to come up with a crazy idea like that?" He has given me the title of *"Disrupter of the Status Quo."*

The great thing about keeping my Friend Balloon inflated with him is that it also keeps my Adventure and Mental Balloons afloat. It allows me to contribute my strengths and talents in a partnership that can achieve far more than I could ever hope to do on my own. Also it keeps me young.

Ernie the Disrupter, Ohio

It All Began At The "Rock-a-Thon"

I always wanted a sister, but no luck. When I was fourteen, God gave me Margaret instead.

We met at a youth group "rock-a-thon" and spent twenty-four hours of the most important hours of our lives rocking together. Little did we know, that event would shape our lives. Our conversations centered on a boy we both liked—or didn't like—or maybe used to like. Anyway, he was history, but we remained together.

Who would have thought that two silly and immature high school girls were about to begin a lifelong journey together? We roomed together in college and got an apartment afterward. As I have gotten older, met people, and observed many lives and friendships, I realize what an unusual friendship we have and what a priceless gift we have in each other.

We went to different high schools. I taught Margaret how to drive in the cemetery across the street from her house. We were in a Bible study and youth group and tried created havoc and adventure wherever we went. My family took Margaret on college visits with us, and we both chose to attend a really small school in Wilmore, Kentucky. Rooming together at Asbury University, we shared the same friends and some more mischievous adventures.

Margaret married, and while she was on her honeymoon, I met my husband. I moved two hours away from her after I married, but distance did not change our bond. We had our first children, both girls, within six weeks of each other. When my daughter was recently married, her daughter was a bridesmaid.

I was there for the birth of her second child, and she was there when I left for Russia to adopt my third child. Our families have taken vacations together, and we have spent every New Year's Eve together for twenty-five years.

Margaret and I have a mutual love and respect for each other that has been the glue of our friendship. I have to say she is my best friend and also one of my heroes—someone

I deeply admire, and someone I am honored to have as a friend.

Kim, Carmel, Indiana

Chapter Thirteen The Physical Balloon

Years ago, I made a mistake with my physical balloon when I created my purpose statement: *"To stay in relatively good shape."* It doesn't take long to realize the flaw in my choice of words.

When I tried to figure out why I couldn't shed those pounds I wanted to lose, I searched out the definition of the word, *relative: In relation, comparison, or proportion to something else.* Therefore, my standard could then be based on anything and anyone I wanted. Thus, for many years, I accomplished my stated purpose—but I know that I never really wanted to pay the price for the health I desired.

A Physical Balloon can go in many directions—and it has been suggested by some health experts we should consider a few things when seeking priorities for our personal health plans.

- Optimal body weight
- Enhanced well-being and mood
- Lower risk of chronic disease

Physical well-being can include weight, diet, exercise plan and consummation habits, but probably the most important thing for us to consider is our mindset. Part of the mindset is about the amount of time that we are willing to invest in our own health. Do we have enough time invested in this? (As in, is your balloon on the floor?) Or is it possible that we invest too much time?

I recently saw a poster with an attractive young lady posing with the caption: "A one-hour workout is only four percent of our day." Ever since seeing the poster, I have used it as my motivation to remind myself that I really am never too busy to workout—it is just that I can find countless other things to do with that four percent of the day.

Thinking back over the years, I see how my Hobby Balloon had a great impact on my Physical Balloon. Beginning in high school as a runner, I continued on as an adult, running in local road races and eventually a marathon, and it was my primary way of maintaining my weight and being in much better than "relatively good shape." I've also had seasons of bike riding and working out at the gym and the obvious results of being in "relatively good shape."

We often hear of the impending national crisis with obesity of children and adults, and one can only wonder if and how that will be reversed. One of the key components to success in creating our own purpose statements is not to copy everyone else's, but in our culture it is hard to ignore all the media messages of not only what our bodies should look like, but also ways to attain the look.

I happened to be at to our local YMCA on January 2nd. I was amazed to see that there was a line to sign in on this particular day. I smiled as I asked the receptionist what was up. Did I miss something? *"It is always like this the first week of the year—just wait a few weeks and it will be back to normal,"* she said.

> "According to the surgeon general, obesity today is officially an epidemic; it is arguably the most pressing public health problem we face, costing the health care system an estimated $90 billion a year. Three of every five Americans are overweight; one of every five is obese. Because of diabetes and all the other health problems that accompany obesity, today's children may turn out to be the first generation of Americans whose life expectancy will actually be shorter than that of their parents."
>
> *Michael Pollan, The Omnivore's Dilemma*

How Do We Help Young People In America?

I have watched, though, as countless young people have been pushed into extracurricular activities year-round to the point that the children are living up to their parents' expectations more than their own. I credit myself as a good learner in this area through the lesson I learned as I coached my daughter's first grade soccer team. Embedded in my brain is this *"Kodak moment!"*

Picking Flowers vs. Playing Soccer

In the middle of the game I noticed that we were one person short on our defensive team and wondered what had happened. On a second look over the field, I saw Andrea sitting down and my first thought, of course, was, what happened? How did she get hurt? On my second look, though, I realized that there was nothing wrong, but instead Andrea had made a decision that picking and studying some of the flowers she had found in the field was more interesting than the game. Obviously, she wasn't keeping her eye on the ball, so she had time to find the flowers.

What is a coach, especially the father of the daughter not caring about the game, to do, other than laugh? Being the genius that I am, I was able to put this in perspective, and it has lasted me my entire life. That was a landmark day for our family.

We realized that the Olympics were no longer in our future with Andrea. We realized that sports might just be a thing we are involved with for social interaction, snacks at half time, and, of course, flower expeditions. If parents could only be realistic about why and what we expect our children to do, life would be so much easier. In our quest for helping our young people with health and fitness, we must help them explore what will work for them.

Growing up for me was so different than what I see today. My parents had this crazy idea that we should *"go out to play and find something to do."* This was not a negotiable value in my home.

Since air conditioning was not yet a common thing, and the wind chill factor was not yet front page, national news, nothing could prevent me from going out of the house. Looking back, I am so thankful for these times because I think this is where some of my creativity and resourcefulness came into action. I often wonder if my parents would be labeled "abusive" as I was allowed to ride my bike just about anywhere that my energy would take me—and even without a helmet! Their expectations were simple: stay out of trouble and do not be late for dinner!

How Does Play Fit Into The Physical Balloon?

The following are questions that I use in my parenting workshops. I explain that many of them are just "old school" ideas—but things that families should wrestle with.

- Has "parental competition" sent families into a habit of overscheduling activities for their kids? Are we're depriving children of times of freedom and character building by not letting them play outside with friends?

- Have our neighborhoods turned into little more than supervised dormitories?

- Are hectic sports schedules damaging our families?

- Should kids wait until they are eleven or twelve to join team sports?

- If kids grow up playing pickup games with no parent or other coaching, do they develop greater passions and instincts for the game?

- Do hectic schedules result in poor meal planning?

- Are we turning children into couch potatoes?

The Evolution Of Our Balloons

While writing this book, I began a new season within my own life. I was able to institute a fitness incentive plan with our showpig.com team.

- The goal: To encourage any type of physical exercise in the upcoming year.

- The strategy: Keep track of your workout sessions of 20 minutes or more in a day. Anything counts!

- The reward: One dollar for each session—paid in full on your birthday!

- The results: After three months we are gaining momentum each week—and each month.

And since I have heard that leadership is about leading by example, I probably lead the team in the number of days to date. This has been a great time and a great reason to reexamine my own purpose statement and am now finally able to proclaim a new one, *"I'm Giving Up Some Things so I can Gain Everything,"* taken from the singer Lecrae.

I'm Giving Up Some Things so I can Gain Everything

To finally make the decision to rethink my purpose statement four months ago has proved to be a great thing. I did not say an easy thing, but a great thing. I started going to the YMCA with a goal of going two to three times a week and have now increased it to three or four a week, with the difference now just being my attitude. I still have the same one hundred and seventy hours in a week—but now I look forward to going and can find the time. I asked Sherri if she would help with my food choices at home, and we have decreased our eating out drastically. What I needed more than the weight loss was the change in vision.

Recently, I went to a conference where the speaker ended his talk with some motivational ideas for getting things done. He explained that "working hard" does not equate to success. I know for myself I do work hard and I like to work hard—both on physical and mental projects. His concluding words, though, helped me better understand my own changing attitude. He said, *"You can work as hard as you want, but if you don't have the right vision, you will not succeed."*

And so for me the idea of *"giving up some things"* might mean things like changing plans to make sure I work out—or maybe giving up that dessert so that I can "gain everything." What I continue to see with the balloons is that so many of them are interconnected. I know that when I work out I eat less, I think more clearly and I sleep better. I know that when I eat less, I have more energy—I chip away at the pounds and I wear the clothes I want to wear.

What excited me about people thinking and rethinking their Health Balloon is that there is not a set way to do it. Sherri is a vegetarian, and it really works for her. I know I eat less meat because of that—not that I am opposed to meat—but because we combine our shopping and cooking choices. What we are finding with the showpig.com team is that they are running, swimming, walking at lunch, doing farm chores, shoveling snow, treadmills, dancing and doing aerobics—and it all works. Each person sets his or her own agenda: how many days a week or month. Some use a scale to check their progress; others check their clothes size. Our success, though, will not be the number of pounds lost or even the number of dollars awarded—the success will come with a new mindset of not being alone in this journey for those who enjoy some support and encouragement along the way. We are not flaunting the results—we want each person's journey to be personal, and for everyone to be able to just share successes and struggles along the way.

I have Always Had A "Skinny Balloon"

I'm not ashamed to admit it—I've always wanted to be thin. And for most of my life that balloon floated along with very little attention from me. I fell blessed to be tall and always enjoyed being active. However, as I aged and had children, that balloon started to deflate. It was a slow, gradual deflation so I didn't even notice it. Until one day it was completely empty. It's not that I ended up extremely overweight; instead I ended up extremely out of shape.

So I started the process of filling that balloon back up. Through years of educating myself on physical activity and diet, my balloon filled but it also evolved. It went from my Skinny Balloon to my Physical Fitness Balloon. The goal is no longer to be thin but to be healthy. This is my body, the vessel that takes me through this life. And it's the vessel that cares for those I hold most dear to me. Where would my family be if I weren't able to care for them? I get one turn around this world with my husband and three sons, and I owe it to them and to myself to feel good, look good and be an active participant in everything we do. That is not possible if I am not healthy.

This balloon is one of my top priorities because it affects so many of my other balloons. And just as important, it affects the balloons of those I love most. I am responsible for what my family eats, and when I make healthy choices, my children take notice. When I set aside time every day for physical activity instead of working overtime, my children take notice. And what's truly incredible is not only do they notice, they joined me. The influence I have over the lifestyle and habits of my family never cease to amaze me.

So how does the wife of a husband who works a full-time job and coaches, has three boys and owns her own business fit in the exercise and cooking required maintaining a healthy lifestyle? I continue to educate myself on the importance of maintaining a healthy body and then finding food and activities that interest me. Then, I plan and build those items into my everyday schedule. And I mean every day. No excuses. And when I find something I love (whether it's a recipe or an activity), I share it. I share it with my family, friends, people I work with - anyone who will listen.

Ami the Mortgage specialist, Cincinnati, Ohio

The Next Steps

Whether building a pyramid, a skyscraper or the house next door, you can't complete it in a day. Embracing the balloons is a building process. Some things to consider:

- Name your own balloons. Mine are mine—and a starting point to get people thinking and processing.

- Be willing to learn, seek counsel and gather ideas of what your balloons could look like—but never believe your balloons should look like your coach's, mentor's, spouse's or friend's—learn to say yes and no to other people's ideas.

- Begin by processing the bigger balloons—the things that are working—and avoid the deflated balloons for a while. Examine why they are your bigger balloons, or see if they really are effective in helping you live the life you want to live.

- Believe in the need for balance in your balloons—perhaps not mastering every single balloon, but becoming passionate in the belief of how necessary each of them is.

- Never imagine that all balloons must grow, mature or be the same size during any season of your life.

- Steal wisdom whenever you can. Do not think you need to re-create everything—resources abound.

The Vision Of The Ten Balloons Is More Than Some People Want

I continually meet parents who will travel to an athletic, sports, music, cheerleading event for an hour, watch the event for two hours, then drive home, having invested four hours of their precious day in their child. Yet, if I would invite them to a two-hour parenting workshop on the *"Ten Balloons and Their Children,"* they would explain that they are too busy to attend.

New learning, new vision for life, is hard work. Laziness might be an issue at times—but I think the bigger truth is our priorities are shaped by our culture. More parents believe they are good parents if they keep their children competing in every aspect of their lives. Fewer parents are willing to be the best parent possible for their own child.

Recently, I heard a motivational speaker address the issue of success, and his emphasis was on the idea that a work ethic and the ability to work hard is not the formula to success. He explained hard work without vision is hard work. I believe as you set out to evaluate your life and the balloons, that is hard work. The value of wrestling with all of the balloons is that it is countercultural. I learned from Zig Ziglar in 1976 that only 3% of adults set goals in all area of their lives—and, of course, even fewer, about 1%, will accomplish them. When I heard this, I determined that I would not only be in the 3%, but in the 1%, and so I am thankful for making that decision. It changed my life. I already knew how to work hard—but I was not always sure what I was working toward. Instead of seeking out what I really needed to do, I took advantage of the things presented to me. Since then, one of the most important things I have learned and embraced is to "Learn to say no to good ideas—and save my yes for the best ideas." Doing that has changed my life and thinking completely.

How Do The Ten Balloons Become A Lifestyle?

The good news is that thousands of books are available to help with each balloon: from fitness coaches, college classes, diet workshops, and on and on—this book is **not designed** to help you live each balloon, but instead to point out the joy, fun and advantages of living a fuller life.

When I began teaching industrial arts in 1969, it was tradition that students made cutting boards and a pump lamp. I realized that junior high students didn't need a pump lamp or a cutting board— and our curriculum changed to making Ethan Allen-type furniture, rowboats, motorboats and canoes for the river in the school's backyard. I didn't realize it then, but I changed the culture of the classroom and the vision of the students forever. As a youth pastor our group served locally over 100 days a year in neighboring communities as well as on national and international mission trips each year—that, for sure, was a change in culture compared to the pizza parties, games and fun agendas that are often the focus within our youth ministry world. I realized that when you change the culture, you meet the real needs of people.

- <u>I realize most people fear change.</u> It is easier for most to do what they did yesterday. Doing what we did yesterday usually requires less resistance than trying to convince others of new ideas. And so the challenge for embracing the Ten Balloons is hard.

- <u>I believe anything is possible.</u> The reason I need a month each year to rethink my purpose statements is that I can be influenced and distracted by many things out there. Most people I know are too "busy and important" to take the time to care for themselves and those closest to them.

Like the example of the parents at the athletic event: growing up, the culture was different for me. I was in three school sports and the summer swim team, and my parents might have seen me practice or compete one or two times. Not per season—but in total. When I tell that story to today's parents, they want to judge my parents. For me it was the best thing ever. They never sat in the classroom or the shop lab with me or went on dates with me. Why would I ever need them to help coach me? As an athlete my goal was always to *"get in the newspaper,"* and then they could read about it if they wanted. They were working parents, and methods of parenting were different then—they wanted me to be responsible, committed and passionate about things and life. They didn't tie it to my GPA or how many trophies I had on my shelf.

- <u>For most to embrace the balloons means to change the culture.</u> I think people need to think about what they need, and maybe what their family needs, based on who they are, not what the media, educational, political and faith cultures say. They need to ask themselves who they want to be. For people of faith, they need to believe that faith is a part of every balloon.

- <u>Process, process, process.</u> Whether you do it by yourself of with others, life needs to be looked at backward and forward. We need to always see where we have been, where we are and where we are going.

Epilogue by Angelia Ham

When I was in high school, I had a job at a local fast food restaurant. For birthday parties I dressed as a clown and made balloon animals. Hey, it was a nice break from taking orders and fielding complaints on the front line. I can still make some of those balloon animals! This was my first memorable encounter with balloons.

I was working as a Youth Ministry Director in my late twenties when I met Mike and later attended his leadership training, where I gained an entirely different perspective on balloons and how they applied directly to my life. I began setting goals for these areas of my life and looking for ways to create overlap between my family, adventure, health and career. Also, I began to see my faith, as something that permeated and flowed throughout my passions, rather than a separate balloon that needed tending to in its own space and time. My faith was no longer one category among many; it was the helium that gave my balloons lift and fullness.

As I was learning to create balloon animals, I had to start over several times on the same creation. I would carefully restart the process, sometimes untwisting several balloons that had been intertwined. Occasionally, a balloon would simply burst and I would start over with a new balloon. Sometimes it was my own fault, sometimes it was someone else's fault and once in a while, there was no rational explanation as to why it popped, but no matter what, I was starting over. It's similar to holding down the "*ctrl, alt* and *del*" buttons on a computer and forcing the computer to shut down and restart. Sometimes in life the balloon pops, the restart is triggered, but it is left to us to initiate the process, to untwist, rebuild and recreate.

Restart

My parents divorced when I was fourteen: restart. I was in my freshman year of college and became pregnant: restart. I gave birth to my firstborn and he had a craniofacial birth defect requiring special care and multiple surgeries: restart. My second pregnancy resulted in a miscarriage: restart. My husband and I separated and came back together: restart. I imagine you get the point. I also imagine you can insert your own stories of those turning points in your life, those times when one of your treasured balloons burst into a million pieces and changed the course of your life into unchartered waters. Try as we may to put those pieces back together, it's never the same.

After navigating 15 years of marriage (very rocky in the beginning, for sure), graduating with my master's degree, "settling down" in a small community in our "forever home," launching into a promising career field and finally getting two of three children into school, my balloons looked quite remarkable. (Did I mention that child number three also had a craniofacial birth defect? Restart.) Despite all the restarts, my balloons were full of color, a beautiful and perfect bouquet of life, surrounded by blue skies, a warm sun and a gentle breeze. One day, everything changed.

I received a phone call that forever altered my life. Almost three hours from home, working at a teen camp for my job, I was awakened in the middle of the night to hear my husband's voice, nearly drowned out by the sound of an ambulance siren, *"Something has happened to Kenny. You need to come home."* I raced home to the local hospital and walked into the emergency room. *"I'm Kenny Ham's mom,"* I told the nurse at the desk. The doors opened, and as I entered the room he was in, I collapsed to the floor, willing the unthinkable away, *"No, no, no."* My 14-year-old son, Kenny, had died. Restart.

No, there is no restarting from this. It's not an untwisting or recreating. There's not a slow, steady reboot for this one. I couldn't articulate it at the time, but this was starting from scratch, with less than I ever had before.

It was three long days later, after an autopsy, when my husband and I were told that Kenny had had rare heart defect called arrhythmogenic right ventricular dysplasia. Despite being an avid soccer player and wrestler, he did not display any symptoms. He was a happy, healthy 14-year-old boy, just graduating eighth grade, ready for high school, with two younger siblings who adored him. It has been three-and-a-half years since he died, June 12, 2010.

Imagine a balloon filled with water or shaving cream. When it pops, the water or substance explodes onto the other balloons around it. Honestly, for me it was more of acid, impacting and nearly destroying everything it touched. All of my balloons were dramatically impacted, and my goals were all instantly reduced to one: to keep breathing.

After nearly four years, I still wish I could reverse that devastating moment in my life, but ultimately, I have gained a perspective that I am thankful to have. At the moment of Kenny's death, all my balloons turned black, the skies clouded over and they went adrift in a violent storm of incomprehension and distress. Over time, my balloons have slowly turned from black to various degrees of gray, then slowly into colors, all in different timeframes. I think they are a bit paler in color than before, however, some are gaining strength and taking on fuller and brighter hues. The brightest part is the new addition of a rainbow across the now blue sky, which is full of a promise for the future.

People will ask, "*How do you do it? How do you survive the loss of a child?*" I can't tell you. Healing is a path that each person must measure in his or her own way. I woke up one day and knew that I had to do something different. I knew I was slipping into a vortex of unspeakable pain and anguish, and I didn't want to be there anymore. The first step was for me to find an outlet for my heartache. I embraced the Health Balloon and started running. I would run until I would cry. I needed the physical exhaustion to reach the point where I could let my emotional exhaustion surface, be dealt with, and trudge on. Eventually I grasped and worked on other balloons, yet I slipped back into the darkness many times. I was ready to rebuild some; others I was not ready to change. Those *"other"* balloons became like old rundown houses. No one lived there anymore, but to rebuild was to bury memories and pieces of my life that I desperately wanted to hold on to.

About a year and a half after my son's death I gave up my full-time career. My youngest child was in crisis, trying to deal with the magnitude of losing his brother, combined with his own special needs. I am now a home educator to my children, and I have learned better how to combine my balloons. I have been teaching fitness classes for over two years, I teach classes part-time at the university and my husband and I do the adventure races together. Frankly, my life is barely recognizable compared to what it once was, but that doesn't mean it's worse.

Over the years I have come to realize that while the "restart" is often traumatic and painful, restart also means to revive, regenerate and resurrect. It is where new dreams emerge and take root. The loss is painful beyond compare, but the view from the top of the mountain, once you get there, is breathtaking. It is there you are closest to the rainbow.

My journey with balloons continues.